Cover, photographs, illus.. aions and editing by
Veronika Paul

And of course management....

Grunt

Introduction

The feminist movement in the 1970's by the CIA was Alice Hastings Bradley Sheldon's dream. She created a parallel universe in the Science fiction world where women controlled human life. She was a clinically depressed professor of psychology. One of her books, for example, "Houston, Houston, Do you read?" was certainly written to upset readers with unthinking prejudices about sex, race, and gender rules.

She concentrated on tragic fiction, ecology, the environment, and always wrote of death, just like a good CIA agent. She wrote about men suffering, and she enjoyed it immensely as James Tiptree, Jr. the pseudonym she used most often. In the end she shot herself and her husband, who was a high CIA official.

Our disagreements with Alice and the rest of the CIA is one of the reasons we wrote this book. We don't want an epidemic like homosexuality or lesbianism or any other epidemic to destroy man. We're in this together, to the end.

If man is to man, if woman is to woman where are the children when the eggs are gone. Luciferians fear the Alphas that is why attrition and cloning is their only answer.

The CIA should take another direction, and not concentrate control through party's advertisement, such as the Democrats, "Luciferians".

It's time to tell the Queen of England to get on board because the Rothschild's seem to be. And the Rothschild's naming their bank. The Bank of England...generous.

This book will take you from February 2016 through August 2017 concentrating on the election and post-election. It is a day to day account of how the Democratic "Luciferian Party" was being destroyed by us. We will have no more Alice's as we have clearly pointed out in the following pages.

Franklin Roosevelt made a deal with the Devil in 1933 and the CIA has been trying to enforce it every sense inception.

James King

Grunt

For Hillary Rodham Clinton

trees smell of life long ago, in a place where no one would look to flow, like liquid sugar, running through the perimeters edge, in a time where the souls run through the waters invisible dredge, separated by fears unlikely to succeed, in a world where the flowers are kept from the weeds, they all are the same someone said, he was expelled from heaven, his sentence, living dead, wanting to befriend them , the hour much too late, souls perishing one after another, their minds have met their fate, the universe dances, knowing the true glamor, mankind coming down on us with its ethical hammer, ethics, is how the establishment keeps you down, the rules only apply when they're not around , so if you see the world as small, you must be Lucifer and have it all.........sgt. ice

A guy looked at my Harley and said I wonder how many people could have been fed for the money that motorcycle cost. I replied I am not sure, it fed a lot of families in Milwaukee Wisconsin who built it, it fed the people who make the tires, it fed the people who made the components that went into it, it fed the people in the copper mine who mined the copper for the wires, it fed people in Decatur Il. at Caterpillar who make the trucks that haul the copper ore, I guess I really don't know how many people it fed. That is the difference between capitalism and welfare mentality. When you buy something you put money in peoples pockets and give them dignity for their skills. When you give someone something for nothing , you rob them of their dignity and self worth. Capitalism is freely giving your money in exchange for something of value, Socialism is taking your money against your will and shoving something down your throat that you never asked for.

Sir, we change the subject? There was a bombing in Pakistan. Did anyone hear? The incident was barely covered by RT let alone anyone else. Oh, but Brussels now that is worth covering, really, because in Pakistan, the jihadist insurgents. Said we are targeting Christians. This is holy warrior's way.
Segregating the Muslims from the Christians, letting them know if they associate with Christians, they will suffer.
Barry "Obama" runs around the world in Air Force 1 telling everyone that all is well with Islam and Christians. This plan has back fired. That there will never be a war between Islam and Christians, what he'll do you think this is.
The Clinton Foundation does it support CARE, Muslim Brotherhood, Arab Emirates, by the way Muslim Brotherhood

7

stands for Jihad Fascism collective.

Emails if I am an operative sending NTN, TS, S, or confidential messages to the state department knowing that the message is going to New York I am automatically arrested. It is not what was received, but what was sent. No one had to scrub anything, there is a record of all sent and received messages. This is embarrassing. These last 3 administrations have been corrupt and have shown the beats true colors.

For example. I am sending Intel to an aircraft carrier for support. My Intel goes to a lady lying on the beach sun bathing, all of my messages went to her, and 100 miles away in the jungle we are DOA. Same, same. All the messages that should have gone to the State department went to two people, Hillary and Barry" Obama" to exasperate the situation by doing nothing. Allowing the motivation, anger, self- esteem to flourish overriding the Middle East and northern Africa. Everything was done intestinally; their emails were found out in a totally different area. Judicial watch. What else? Allowing information to go to only Barry and Hillary has ruined the world. On new level. Recent CIA, special CPS trained ISIS to kill Christians

from 1979 Recon Marines trains Al Qaeda continuously. For so many months Fox and everyone was saying why won't Barry stop ISIS. He gave orders to train them. What will happen if Hillary becomes President? On that note, the minute Hillary texted her daughter and told her about the truth. That it was a terrorist attack. At that time her daughter was involved in an international incident. And when the lies where told. She, Chelsea had an obligation to go to the FBI, that s obstruction unlawful detention of justice.

Film man in L.A. You have to understand. We want America to be #1 and everyone else a distant # 2. That is the only way it works. There are 28 idiots in NATO. NATO should be dissolved.

Mr. Trump, sir. They know if you become president, they all will be in orange jump suits and we can expand Guantanamo Bay and now that we have an Embassy... We can put a couple of our bases there, not to mention more Marines. The holy warriors will be coming from everywhere Remember 9/11

Clinton Yugoslavia, flight 800 and Barry well you know Romney took the money, Barry took the white house.

Grunt King, Sgt. ICE Semper Fi

A tainted batch of Norco has killed six people in Sacramento.

Nearly 30 people have overdosed and six people have died in less than a week in Sacramento, California after using a tainted form of a narcotic painkiller being sold on that city's streets.

A batch of the opiate Norco being sold in the California capital appears to have been laced with fentanyl, an opiate that is roughly 100 times more potent than heroin, according to *the Los Angeles Times*.

Grunt King

April 11, 2016 ·

Having a private server can only be ordered by Barry...........Mr. Micromanagement ....you could only come up with a video.....Hillary told the public, same breath, told her daughter it was a terrorist attack. And Barry is behind it all did they tell you that Chris Stevens was also sexually assaulted, sodimized, I hate the gov running the internet. Anyway you see if we would have retaliated, Barry might have to give his noble peace prize away, not to mention the psychological war he has made with the military......all about presentation empty uniform. Now on with this week's chat. Mohammad Hasson Chandoo tony rezko Arab action American network Andy stern the truther girls uses vs.info breadboards footage Jeff Rense and mia pod own lo club Donald young Nate spencer Brokeback Obama no capitalization needed for

a punk Sinclair news.net frank marshal Davis and Barry Soetoro
how to impeach the establishment tomorrow rir

Grunt King

April 14, 2016 ·

a poem for my daughter jenny age 33and 2/3,one day as I was
traveling through time, I stopped to watch the hour less mimes, as I
got caught up in the charade of the day, my mind wandered through
the mountains and seas of yesterday , in and out of space my spirit
moving free, one world after another , being only me, as , I glide
between the stars into the circle of light ,I lose feeling and fall out of
sight, to watch the inhabitants ,is a most blissful thing , only until
they run out of food and water do they feel the sting, one by one ,
planet , by , planet they never feel the ground , to watch them die
day after day they live but never here a sound , it is time to stop and
take a sample of this races sentiments, but soon in a noble setting
you'll all be the queens elaborate migrants , as they divide , the land,
and soon the planets and all their joy, to realize that we are not toys,
we are survivors ,Robots in Space....sgt. ice rir

Grunt King

April 15, 2016 ·

Water of life community church, DVD #1088, guest speaker,
Brigitte Gabriel, Fox News Correspondent, Author and Terrorist
Survivor, Senior Pastor, Dr. Dan Carol. the dvd is called the rest of
the story....'war has been declared on Christians , ...as Islamic
fundamentalism spreads its tentacles worldwide , it is crucial for the
people ...to understand the danger , know what to expect , and know
what to do about it. " Brigitte Gabriel this church is 12.5 miles
away from san Bernardino ca. hey fbi what church did the victim's
go to 16 years, I guarantee 4 more will not happen you want to play
psychological warfare boy by rules of engagement I am just getting
started Barry. We know everything Barry out of the bag it will drop.
senator mc Cain all the marines I know who are not disillusioned by
the establishment wants you gone yesterday and you can take your
fuck'n daughter from fox with you you fucking little cunt let me on

10

the news I dare you what is a matter you afraid of my service dog.
Hey Barry, how many people have died in your administration by
"natural" causes because they not allowed following the
constitution. you are just a little15 year old that should be in a
mental ward, Obama fuck you world committee ....sgt ice
more to come 7 months more Hillary is a murderer I wish Facebook
would not capitalize her name , her daughter did not even call the
fbi after Benghazi . not mi5 mi6 the queens all for it.........we are
patriots , now it is us against the world not just the redcoats......you
kids that grew up on Barry are as ....research
facts if you find them not propaganda come on i have been on this a
month out of almost 60 years you pissed me off Barry Cook Co.
does not like to be upset ....Barry it is not about money , loyalty,
protocol , self-indulgence of Christians dying ......Barry principle
you thought it was just business as usual uh Barry. Go to the
Indiana Dunes relax, go visit the father in Michiana, the bishop
wrong pic for pope........ No all about Argentina sgt ice rir

Adolf Hitler	Bernie Sanders
• Believed state power would fix Germany	• Believes state power will fix America
• Proposed gun control	• Proposes gun control
• Promised a political revolution	• Promises a political revolution
• Called himself socialist	• Calls himself socialist
• Blamed Jews for Germany's problems	• Blames the rich for America's problems
• Wanted a heavily regulated economy	• Wants a heavily regulated economy

Grunt King

I love you all, all my peep's from all over the world. I want to send love out to boy's from Benton park to Gravois 44 to Maryville back when I used to think back and click clack....from St. Louis...........Dear entity of Saudi Arabia.....Ambassador Sheikh gave Basnan 73,000$ for Prince Bandar to pay for his wife's , Princess Haifa Faisal to have a thyroid operation. The money was given to Majeda Dweikat. Al-Bayoumi, Khelid, Alewat, the hijackers met at a restaurant in San Diego .The funds of 73,000$ was released to Al Bayomi after the meeting with the other two. The visa for Al -Bayoumi was extended by Ambassador Sheikh on the same day. Background on Al-Bayoumi: year 2000-Saudi Gov. civil aviation, defense dept.Basnan returned to Saudi Arabia, Dweikat deported to Jordon. The windshield cowboy said job well done. It would have taken years, if ever for this to happen. To start the beginning of a 3rd world war. Shame on you Do you remember flight 800. Bill Clinton had a missile launched from a sub, destroying the plane - who was on that manifest? There were hundreds of witnesses; the FBI called them all a liar. All the same, probably Hillary's idea...I wish they would not capitalize her name. The white house and I do mean it's the whitest it's ever been, unfortunately have housed many terrorists over the years by their own description. I have a t -shirt that say's been fighting terrorists since 1492, being truly part Indian, I felt it appropriate. Do you wonder why no one wanted jeb bush to run, let alone win ....we like is Kennedy Center. During the bush administration the democrats, headed by Mr. Schumer wanted the letters opened. Sen. Sam Brownback R. of Kansas voted against it. Now the Republicans want the letters, and Barry is against it. What a shock.........he has been to Saudi Arabia more than any other president. It is called world domination. I forgive American trained guerillas for doing what they do. who trains guerillas by the dozens , sends them off to kill their cousins , the CIA man , the fucking CIA man....Who can take sugar from a sack , fill it with LSD and put it back , the CIA man ,fucking CIA man.....Who had a meeting with God took his staff , then took his Rod , the CIA man , the fucking CIA man.......my ptsd shakes , and baby seizures , sweating

12

has taken over .....With the new law here they can storm the house shoot my service dog, my caregiver and me. Washington is one of the largest terrorist organizations in the world................time to go back to the Jungle. ....Take it away families.............Sgt. Ice rir

for the children , and the low heeled sparks from high heeled boys , walking through the forest , quietly ,not to wake anyone up , the sky is forever blue in the summer , feeling the warmth of earth Mothers love , walk turning into a run , ah.............the sound of a glacier fed brook , must have another cup , flowers of color , so bright ,and full of spring life , playing , spinning , looking up , falling , down , aroma of soft green grass , mother was pleasant , everything grew , without a strife ,as I approach the Cliffside now I am in tears , for there is no water mass , sitting down, wiping the tears of an Indian away , a crack of a smile ,eyes illuminating , Chiefs all knowing , only a few , have chosen to stay , but what is the saddest part of all , using global warming as an excuse for imminent domain, been fighting terrorists since 1492........sgt. ice rir.........a little something for my peeps......................TalismanicIdols.org...

April 24, 2016 ·

Agenda 21...............knowledge rules..

Grunt King

April 20, 2016 ·

Politics is a paid illusion. there is only one God...............you will pay , politician , for the illusion and false narrative , you have given to the people , when God looks down upon you , there will be no excuses...........through the gates of Hell you will go.....can't wait to see you in an orange jumpsuit , Barry , Obama , Hillary............if you want the Muslim brotherhood ,collective j-had factions , the Saudi caliphate , the families of the 1936 meetings , China ,and of course ultimately behind it all , the queen.... if trump wins u.k. dies . Doe's anyone watch the RT channel 280 here, the Kiser report.........my friends and I had this figured out a long time ago. and when we looked forward 8 years ago with my bud Ray in Maui.........it was , easy writing on the wall.........rir is taking you down nothing but money grubbing traders........any Barry we are just getting started.............hang on ....you are about to start losing your gray hair. Ambassador Sheikh rings a bell...

Grunt King

Princess Rourou......palm tree , undecided , yet drawn , to the trumpets in the sky , sun ever ending , in a way the palm grows bye and bye, houses still come and go , but the shadows of palm , so cheerful , so bright ,into the bedroom of homes comforting children always, their dreams into the night , sing with me ,be with me forever, palm nature adorns and wraps her wet love , green grass beckoning for the stabilization and hope yearning for the white dove , seagulls mesmerized by the earth laid soul of the palm to be , nature has a way of telling us the true meaning of wisdom so we may see , there you go , and there you are , never tired , always giving your best , palm tree against southern California skies di bo Chet sgt. Ice

Grunt King

The ultimate Global Hug
The U.N. failed to achieve even one of the eight Millennium Goals by 2015. And the man in charge of making it happen knew it was a lost cause
for those of you at the news stations that did not understand Mr. Trump let me break it down..........
In 2006 I was invited to debate the issue of the United Nations before the Cambridge Union at England's Cambridge University. one of the individuals was debating was the director of the U.N's Millennium Project, which had been created in 2000 to " create a global partnership to reduce extreme poverty" That mission, according to the United Nations was to accomplished through eight specific goals focusing on the areas of poverty, hunger, diseases and education.
Just before we were to enter the debating chamber I turned to him and said" You realize you don't have a prayer, don't you?"

I replied, "Ending poverty through redistribution of wealth". He replied, "Yes, I know". Then we headed into the debate.
Over the weekend of September 25 to 27, 2015, at the U.N. headquarters in New York City (just as in the 1992 U. N. Earth Summit in Brazil, thousands of delegates, U.N. diplomats, representatives of nongovernmental organizations, 193 heads of state, and the pope converged to unanimously adopt a new 15 year plan entitled" Transforming Our World: the 2030 Agenda for Sustainable Development". The 17 goals outline
Goal: 1 End poverty in all its forms everywhere.
Goal 2 End hunger, achieves food security, improve nutrition, and promote sustainable agriculture. These two items translate to redistribute of wealth and control of food production, U.N. documents go into great details on controlling food supplies. As for elimination of poverty, it is interesting to note that nothing is mentioned about providing a means for the poor to own private property so that they can climb out of poverty.
Goal 3 Ensure healthy lives and promote wellbeing of everyone at all ages. This means cradle to grave control of what we eat and how we live. The healthy lives they promote means walking and riding bikes as we live in controlled high rise apartment buildings.
Goal 4 Ensure inclusive and equitable quality education and promote lifelong learning opportunities for all. We learned a long time ago that lifelong learning is only necessary as a means to continually apply behavior modification practices to assure we maintain the desired attitudes, values and beliefs to live in a global village.
Goal 5 Achieve gender equality and empower all women and girls. The White House is bathed in rainbow colors, meanwhile the government moves to embrace Sharia law and its war on women.
Goal 6 Ensure availability and sustainable management of water and sanitation.
Goal 7 Ensure access to affordable, reliable, sustainable and modern energy for all.
Goal 8 Promote sustained, inclusive and sustainable economic growth, full and productive employment and decent work for all.
At the end Mr. Trump said No to the Agenda 21.and in my own words not his. He told the Queen to shove it. Personally I hope and pray this last year. Are the Bushes dead yet? You fuckan Demons.
Sgt. Ice RIP Story by Tom De Weese

.

15

Grunt King

April 27, 2016

Hold on to your hats boy's, don't you love her madly, want to be her daddy, you want love her as she's walking out the door.........................tell, me what you say..............the DOORS

Grunt King

April 28, 2016 ·

Don't show up here..............kids we are real men, with real love for our country, you grew up with Barry. Obama the 15 year old who did not get enough love from his mommy...................you are brainwashed socialists, communists, fascist's .not your fault. That was the way it was supposed to be starting with 1936...........meeting of the minds.......grow up......the kid that graduated said he, they did not know what their job was...like Nancy Pelosi...the cunt sad about healthcare.......when we were in boot camp before our Rifle Prayer, we were told to kill all Muslim insurgents and communist insurgents.......................................that was in the 70's....they know exactly what they want you to do in every situation.....you have the iq of what a bubble...........for my friends I mean no offense , I was 17.........it I the point I am trying to make , nothing is done without knowing the outcome...........sgt ic rir

Grunt King

April 28, 2016 ·

Don't show up here..............kids we are real men, with real love for our country, you grew up with Barry...Obama the 15 year old who did not get enough love from his mommy...................you are brainwashed socialists , communists , fascists .not your fault . That was the way it was supposed to be starting with 1936...........meeting of the minds.......grow up......the kid that graduated said he, they did not know what their job was...like Nancy Pelosi...the cunt sad about healthcare.......when we were in boot camp before our Rifle Prayer, we were told to kill all Muslim insurgents and communist insurgents.....................................that was in the 70's....they know exactly what they want you to do in every situation.....you have the iq of what a bubble..........for my friends I mean no offense , I was 17.........it I the point I am trying to make , nothing is done without knowing the outcome..........sgt ic rir

This is the Border Fence Mexico built on their border with Guatemala to keep out freeloaders. Notice The Barbed Wire & Towers with Armed Guards. Shouldn't the United States have the same right as Mexico to protect its border?

For you Californians, if you like communism, socialism, fascism then vote for cunt Hillary or Bernie, you must have the iq of a 100....why don't you go back to work ...oh...I am sorry you don't have any job to go to.......Barry Obama made sure of that ....bush made sure of it Clinton made sure of it....Barry the ambassador will pay the families of 9/11.....oolong with the prince , princess of everyone that was involved.....we know everything game over.....and we do not want Hitler's youth, and pol pot....and his beautiful killing machine the children......fema...what a fuk'n joke...Trump will be the next president of the United States.........you vote for Cruz you vote 4 Monsanto, they will destroy the pollen , everything will be man-made ...they have stolen Gods staff. Every nutrient will be controlled. the transformation started taking place in 2012....it is called attrition ...if this is staged by Barry....or the weather underground.................this is not Lebanon I will not say this again.....the average I q in this group is 140.......they would like to tell you it does not matter.....look at yourselves.....what's a matter are you afraid he will actually supply real jobs and you would have to work.....drama , British lit , Greek drama civics, trig....calc 1and 2...no we are not the fucking same...this country according to my passport book is a socialist , fascist ...directing the fault to Barry Obama ....Barry Obama just wants everything recorded for when the hammer comes down especially for you that got married "same sex" is now recorded. Laws to pick up terrorists that are law abiding citizens that know and disagree , just like Mr. Trump....I have been to so many 3rd world shitholes.....and this better not be one of them....you probably do not even know what agenda 21 is you poor dumb cool aide drinking bastards.....Barry ...we want you to resign now ...we want you and bush tried for War crimes.....this is not Lebanon love my peeps this for Barry , the boy that masturbates to Christians dying you are a sick fuck . George Soros's his job is to kill countries...eh found someone who hated the U.S. more than him...by the way...this is for Michelle ....I used to tutor black kids.....for the type of schools..............one was a pimp he gave his main girl for tutoring...........................he was shot by gang members from Chicago....this was during integration ....by blacks into white schools ......we went into the world shocked.......our school is gone.............this was a result of films being shown on the media...............the media elects the politicians here....that is why they are so cocky..............grow up realize we are much brighter than you ....competition baby.........I cannot type worth a shit but you Earl you know ,the guy that designed the electronic functions of the Space Shuttle, we used to work in the same office at Pt.Mugu ....propaganda ....that the people that vote 4

18

Mr. Trump......make under 50,000...blue collar.....when you get out to Cali.......us old 60's and 70's Vet's just may surprise you Megan.....................we know that Karl Rowe and Dana Perino have their lips permanently sewn to the bushes genitals ....we old fucks have been at this for 3 wks. I have not typed since 99...imagine what it will be like in Nov. you have misleading the people not us since conception ......for God's. Kick Barry and Hillary in the balls so hard that they cannot get up.....establishment...you are busted ....when it came between Mr. Trump and Hillary......what you girls thought..................p.s. I used to bend spoons, make paper clips fly , pencils role ...you know barely thinking......and you are complacent ....the Gentleman and Officers , Senior Enlisted , Enlisted have lost their lives for freedom...the Heroes are in the ground.......keep insulting our baby boomers....sgt. ice rir

Grunt King

May 2, 2016 ·

To Green Dogs............who were initially responsible for my obtaining Grunt as a Service Dog. and thanks to DR.D of the Stockton V.A that said I was eligible and that I must have a Service Dog for life.............this is love , this is understanding , this is compassion ....this is America..................God bless all my peeps .....1/9....C...co...........and all you s.o.b's in scamp...3rd recon.............and 1 true idiot from team 5 Tony D........

Grunt King

May 2, 2016 ·

the life of an amateur ..,the life of a butterfly, beyond the cocoon, what shall we do, with all of this room, blue skies at rainbows end, green upon green, and so it will begin, bark of the trees, so black, so healthy, the earth, if she were money, would be most wealthy, stumbling through the galaxy at 1,000's plus, cannot believe, literally, she holds all of us, the equilibrium and balance, soon to be gone, we can't seem to except this is a live organism we're on, the green and blue object, yet feeling so bright, not knowing, underneath her, an ever ending light, heat, growing intense under oceans, without a sound, water, getting warmer, until the fish are run aground, and not to mention the rocks in the sky, so bend over

world, and kiss your ass goodbye.................sgt. ice
rir...........................

Grunt King

to the Pentagon , you still there bobby....................you know what to
do..........swing the lobbyist your way.......it must be hard with all of
your well laid plans.........you know you don't like Barry..........if you
do ,and you are associated with him under....................look.
Jerusalem ...had not been for the illuminati ....might still be a
Kingdom to look for peace...and Monsanto; please...I have seen
your op...in St. Louis.....sigma please ....we are about to have a blast
from the past......so exit the illuminati and peace shall reign
...................for my Brothers and Sisters, and General Austin
Murray....................we are and have been so
proud.........silence.........leathernecks
only...from the halls of Montezuma, to the
shores of Tripoli: we will fight our countries battles.....in the air, on
land, and sea: first to fight for right and freedom.............and to keep
our honor clean:, we are proud to claim the title......of united states
marine...our flag's unfurled to every breeze....from could take a
gun;. In the snow of far off northern lands. And in sunny tropic
scenes, you will find us on the job...the united states
marines........here's both to you and our corps...which we are proud
to serve:....in many a strife we've fought for life. And never lost our
nerve...if the army and the navy ever look on Heaven's scenes, they
will find the streets are guarded ....by United States
Marines.........Hymn ....Sgt. Ice rir

Grunt King

people you may know......Adam weishof, Rothschild's, covenant of
golden dawn, order of illuminati , enlightened one, supreme order,
nesta Webster, masons and illuminati, alliance official, comet de
virive, john doe-brit mi5 taught black magic to Liz 2 of England,
king George funded both sides of the revolution..I.r.s collects taxes
for Brittan from England and the united states....notice capital letters
for England only.........I will talk about that at a later date.........we

have shares in the IRS...Nasa CIA etc. we do not own them....un assigns soc #'s through IMF .John Brown...Rothschild dynasty, .Wilson league of nations, income tax unconstitutional.......our money goes to the central fed.non-gov....owned. Suspension of species payment.........Gov. theft.............they do not have to pay it back ....they will assign 15 trillion in land to china for example..........there is no deficit your souls have already been sold...ask Hillary and Barry Obama................sgt.ice rir

Grunt King

May 11, 2016 ·

House Speaker Paul Ryan is not affiliated with the illuminati, trilateral commission, or Bilderberg group ....8 years ago he was ok......8 years is a long time......Presidential Nominee Donald Trump should ask these questions first.........avoid any future complications..........................I have list ...so let's see what Paul says...................the.3 tried to stop him from .educating students on politics.............they said ...they did not want the students to know their future.................if he is clean...he should be the Vice president.................that way the people........will have a chance to live without a 3rd world war. That has already started..........15 years ago. Are destiny decided in36.again in 92 Brazil.............again when Westfield's Marriott.........Catelli Virginia closed to weeks for the Bilderberger group.........C.I.A......mi-5-6...it is built in the center of the military complex...125 of the richest demons in the world that are stuck on the 19 and 20 century.......this the 21 century..............America 1st..Period ...that way no nuclear holocaust.................no exterminating 6 billion people.........no Monsanto nutrients that already been implemented..................oh yes...there were two demon's Hillary and Barry Obama also present..............once again .they decided and Barry walked away with it henry Kissinger his mentor out of law school said he would be good in a crisis..............for you black lives matter............even know your puppets or educated communists ...I doubt it .anyway. Listen to KRS ONE. In the green room in Austin Texas...he said .that the Bilderberg group................that is the correct spelling...the reason we did this is KRS ONE explained the entire process of the selection of Barry. Using burgers and fries....................at the Marriott they had a fire drill and everyone had to leave but the artificial elite.............I will have much more this week and to my peeps at ppp........no one will get the bomb as long as Presidential Nominee Donald is President..............he is not associated with these groups.......he is trying to save us .not kill us Barry was trained by henry Kissinger and many communists........there are over 100 communists in the house and senate........time to clean house......sgt. ice rir

Grunt King

May 11, 2016 ·

to the low healed sparks of high heeled boy's............with love comes pain sometimes knowledge provides pain.............also.............to my peeps in St. Louis ....got a beat ....chorus...........hey little Barry, we're not messing around...........count to 10 ....jump.........and put our pimp hand down....my boy's the St. Lunatics...finish it up ...I'll do it you fella's rap it.........and I will throw in some of that lead guitar............blues it up. Robert Johnson isn't the only one that sold his soul for the blues.............at the cross roads of time.....but he was my father's favorite........my father said he would never make it.........I ask why. He said he was sent from God.......Martin Luther King..............that is.....a song for the family.......................chorus.............I feel alright tomorrow, I feel alright today, but I am going down there, and getting myself killed anyway,.......upon the earth, I will eventually strip.........all there artificial powers, ego and leadership...do not come to sorrow, or even worry my Son,....you will not see it coming, until their evil deed is done.........one day my Father, to the Universe of its own,. One day my father, I will be upon the throne,...and if I am to have children, dear Father, what then do I say....knowing that they're going to die, Father,...when I send them away........chorus........titled Self Sacrifice................there is no room for the mystery religion in our Bible or Constitution.............sgt ice rir.........

Grunt King

May 19, 2016 ·

To my peeps, .low heeled sparks of high heeled boy's............I love you all.........I can hardly see through the tears, of others............because they can't see at all through their own tears. But, let's say we take the time.....off the cuff...to all the humans that wanted to be , all humans that wanted to see, the children, that did not have a chance, to live a life, and have romance, I wonder what was on their mind, when they were so close, but left behind, I wonder when they hit the water, had their soul left their chest, was it because of a name on a manifest, in a blink of an eye, the souls went straight through the sky, and said one last goodbye, and to this earth they shall return, to help fight the demons of our concern, you may have a Dome, and we have a steeple, most of us want peace, we are God fearing people...............sgt..ice rir

to my peeps, and the low heeled sparks of high heeled boy's.................there is two parties in America.....................The American Party,..........and the COMMUNIST PARTY.........how does it feel to have your PARTIES name in CAPITOL letters bitch..........remember......fed reserve......non species payment.............the cunt of the year besides Hillary longshank is Madame Christine laggards............check out.....www.agorafinancial.com.............it is not Nov. yet Barry......................George ...you might want to do a 360..........put our towers back in place. Drop the IMF...micromanagement...seems to be the theme these days...........drop china elements of Europe, keep Japan............or kill America, or keep china. Keep Europe........bla..bla...bla...........we want our stock market back.............your fired bitch.............remember ....p.p.p......................work together.................we are at the finish line.....been sitting here since 2008..........these are demons.....eyes wide shut...the 9th gate.....................these are movies they show a segregation ....in detail latter....medicine time.........love you all ....thank all of you that has accepted Grunt and I your friend to agree to disagree...a oh bears coming...tired and strumming.......down the park and kicking it down, then I look around, and see, her looking at me, the sky is blue, everything is through,.......blunt on the table, she rolled up and felt stable, I fired it up, she didn't smoke, broke out a vapor, and

23

begin to toke,......I said hey honey what's the plan,............I shadowed on over to make you a hell of a man.............just like countries..........I would rather fuck than fight...........but hey..........sgt. ice rir.......p.s....there is an F18 pilot on fox........she is a regular.......as Congressman Charlie Wilson............would say.......you can teach them to fly, but you can't teach them to grow Tits..........Charlie 9ner foxtrot.......once again ....shadow stay ahead of target.........................

Grunt King

May 25, 2016 ·

Hillary...............what clearance does your daughter have with the st, dept., ,fbi, c.i.a. Bilderberg group, trilateral comm., the illume........oh...your just a builder.............there should be a citizen's arrest...........Chelsea.........did your daddy tell you to shut up , or was it mommy....or , you are just another demon........so Chelsea , while Ambassador Steven's and others were getting fucked to death.......................you thought that was ok........the concentration is on you ....you fucking demon cunt........you and the Clinton political correctness ....this is not Lebanon...............................this is America. Windshield wiper cowboy........has not forgotten about you.......................

May 25, 2016 ·

Henry Kissinger, in an address to the Bilderberger group meeting...........sometimes Bilderberger is a better way to spell it...............you will see the manager but never the wizard behind the franchise. ....anyway, in Evian, France, may 21, 1992, as transcribed from a tape recording made by one of the Swiss delegates----- ....today Americans would be outraged if U.N. troops entered L.A. to restore order;, tomorrow they would be grateful! This is especially true if they were told there was Hillary...............what clearance does your daughter have with the state, dept., ,FBI, C.I.A. Bilderberg group, trilateral comm., the illume........oh...your just a builder.............there should be a citizen's arrest...........Chelsea.........did your daddy tell you to shut up , or was it mommy....or , you are just another demon........so Chelsea , while Ambassador Steven's and others were getting fucked to

death.......................you thought that was ok........the concentration is on you ....you fucking demon cunt........you and the Clinton political correctness ....this is not Lebanon...............................this is America. Windshield wiper cowboy...has not forgotten about you........................
An outside threat from beyond, whether real or promulgated, that threatened our very existence. It is then that all peoples of the world will plead with world leaders to deliver them from this evil. the one thing everyman fears is the unknown --------when presented with this scenario, individual rights will be relinquished for the guarantee of their wellbeing granted to them by the world Gov. Barry o. was selected out of law school as you know to work for old henry.........remember...blame others for what you do........carl Marx.......was a Satanist. And went to a satanic church..........1970's history class ...you kids have been hammered with misinform................angles...wrote the communist manifesto.................before he died, repented to God. He ask to forgive him for writing the communist manifesto ....I apologize for the type o's ash...good day's bad day's..........sgt.ice rir

Grunt King

May 27, 2016 ·

To my peeps, and low-heeled spark of high-heeled boy's...............say something quick ....CIA trained Muslim insurgents, go to Syria killing 100's of thousands of Christians. Barry o. said it was the JV team because, it had not advanced enough for him...how many Christians did Barry kill. And through rules of engagement...how many people did Barry kill. Through micro management, how many people did Barry and Hillary longshank kill...there is a# ....how many people did bush kill....how many marines and soldiers, 9/11.......have you noticed how quite it has been......the cracker Barry knows........the eyes wide shut crowd , the old ones at the top of the mountain of the movie 300 , with the oracle......with the drones, trained Muslim insurgents, kidnappings, killings, torture to whom, not them, us Christians , Christians are Christians no matter where they are........when Barry walks out of the shithouse you know how many law suites he has? You are the ugliest demon barrack, you are obvious, and the Order will not forgive you. Our military was designed to fight on foreign and domestic soil...you do not need Americore; they are there if only a situation is planned by micro. In other words. Egypt didn't go your way, Syria didn't go your way, gee, I wanted Muslims to rule, I wanted, to shift the power to Iran, look at the map.....news's people, what the hell do you get paid for, or how much do they pay you not to say....everyone knows but you,,,, oh, I have be politically correct or daddy won't pay me. To get to the mystery religion, they have to kill a lot more Christians. brainwash Muslims or threaten them through paperwork....this has been going on since 1936.......the demon Barry left the castle just like Hitler and look what happened ..that is why Barry said,,,,,i could be pres. 4 a third time....I will explain...a county over from is mariposa , the town of mariposa...has delegates that deep 150 years in this town, the man my plumber, ran for sheriff, everyone thought he won, they knew each other...small town...he lost.......the ballets were found later, on the side of a mountain ......my Father said: nothing will change but technology........we will all die before our brain s and body hold true evolution.....con...Barry allows the same Muslim insurgents that were trained by us. He is loving it he is enjoying this...you lose Barry.............and we pray every single night that you and you die just as if you ordered them remember what you said. I will give them my own version of shock and ahhh...you will walk out of the now shithouse and the law will be waiting...I am the one from the....we'll see, said the Zen master...Sgt. Ice rir Sonora VA...san Diego Mexico etc. You are an embarrassment to politics.............................

Grunt King

May 27, 2016 ·

Do you really want to know what California thinks; you will see, good by illegals, from where ever, good-bye sanctuary cities, 'America', good-bye cartel, hello. Immigrants, step right in, after the wall is built, how about Germans, Austrians, Notice how German is kept in small print........women running from sharia law, how about real refugees , the Christians, oh, there already dead and still dying you son of a bitch. Or should I say son of a whore...you are the separator that is for sure, have not had this much dislike since op...........mission............chasing drug dealing. Tycoons, involved with..............you have no class, just hate for us. The pentagon owns

26

50% of the budget, and they are under the same commands from the blt cfr.............we , the people, you do not create situations for attrition...for you artificial black lives matter, you are already a black spot...watch esoteric agenda...beyond zeitgeist......there is some relevant info yellow spots, red spots, farm zones..etc...Agenda 21...........bush...Nafta...the first black pres. Billy...the child lover Clinton.............a. designate men to accomplish the following missions: 1. handcuff, blindfold, search and gag prisoner,2 treat and bandage prisoners wounds, 3. carry or assist him, 4,carry his equipment and weapon,5 cover the telltale signs at the ambush site,6 take care of friendly win's or mia's to include their weapon and equipment, 7take point , rear security and who will be alternate in each......8, make security check of extraction lazy, 9stand guard over prisoner or prisoners at lazy..........these type o's......by the way ,I was not raised this way, the opposite.....some things I remember very well, and I suggest the rest of you do the same.......their coming...............disease, insurgency, americore, pen. Gov. already said what he would do...he said he would do anything to save pen............I do not mind. Sharing with Barry...remember Hillary longshank is the one to watch................ Into the jungle, trees of old have given laughs to satellites...when all you need is your mind.................p.s. on this gender thing. We are all bi...Acting on it is up to you...............sgt ice.rir

Grunt King

June 6, 2016

to all my new friends , I have been away from the table........so to
speak....thank all of you for your friendship and kindness....these are
the greatest bunch of human beings......betcha never thought
becoming human was tour only objective, and what an
objective,........man , do I have a long ways to go...but I am
aware..............heaven cannot afford to grow complacent , and
neither can we.....in heaven, shit, you just roll one up,......on earth,

depends on what sector of the planet you're on, you could be
seriously misrepresented........so being human is a challenge, all
these rules....................unfortunately are a drag...so why don't you
say , let's go ahead and make it legal across the board......no worries
mates..........another type -o ash........sit down ..Yea yea...feel it...here
she comes
walking past me , ever so slow , the smell of her perfume, everyone
knows, she was always there for him, through the battles and scorn,
they could not beat him, his soul was not to be torn, they could not
cheat him, for they would be wrong, they could not defeat him, for
he was to strong.....they could not out talk him, or set a trap, he was
known as the first rapper, with words he could scrap, when he

28

walked into the ring, they could feel his sting, and then came that welcomed sound, when the fighter hit the mat, Ali......had put his pimp hand down............God bless the Champ and his family

Grunt King

June 10, 2016 ·

this is a way to wake up................good morning, low heeled sparks of high heeled boy's.......................it is Friday.......I feel a poem coming.....into the nights we lose our sight, only to be brought back into the light, by common threads, we live alone, so we may not be shown, the threads may stay together, if we are strong, and remember, the world is ours to embrace, we are the human race..........all demons must disappear without a trace...........reality check........if it wasn't for gravity.........sgt. ice rir

Grunt King

June 10, 2016 ·

So Hannity...judge, cnn, abc...cnbc............as far as we are concerned you are all fucking criminals..............and Joe , you should be ashamed...................................there will be no more demons in the shithouse, and little Billy, you can start crying now....we are in charge..believe it..............punk and to all the new friends.............you are the wealth of this world....do not let anyone tell you different.........plus your all beautiful and handsome..............the Intel is through the roof.........we have agreed that God is a mathematics genius , and in this sector......we are concentrated on putting the entire Gov. in jail, last man standing, because she demon, Hillary longshank, and everyone else must be arrested, nato, senate, house, royalty, CIA, fbi, state dept. Bush, Barry bama .....we want a demon political free small Gov. massive military.....for humanitarian reasons.....everyone .is supposed to have a chance.............not just the selected...............they want all of us Christians dead but I will tell the sob of a whore to his face.............after we water board him..........you are going to Cuba for a while...........I was brought up to love everyone ....not demons...........what do they do with pests in America...we........................Sgt. Ice rir

June 12. 2016 ·

fuck you senator, the leader of the manipulative terrorists org is in the senate the house of representatives, the shit house, the Bilderberg group, trilateral commission, illuminati, cfr......or blt-cfr.......over 100 communists in the house and senate.....Bernie was just there to make her look good and she is still a cunt, cunt, cunt----
-----------Hillary longshank that is............we will not have 16 more years of stomping out America...it will not happen.............we train CIA, we train troops, special forces...to train Muslim insurgents, to kill Christians, anywhere in the , you are not the president, you want to be black but you can't........cracker.........demon.....you did not earn that , the blt-cfr said you would be good in a crisis.......a good face for the Bilderberg group.............fuck the "elite" and fuck you........we have the entire list of all of you and President Trump----
---he may not be perfect, but he is American........after the election. We want.......all blt-cfr...........investigated, all members...especially Hillary, Obama, Barry...........bill Clinton ,Condoleezza rice, bill gates, David Cameron, Charles prince of whales, RICK PERRY of tex.timothy Geithner, Lester b. Pearson, henry Kissinger, Colin Powell, john Edwards, prince Philip duck of Edinburg..ha ha.....George Stephanopoulos, queen Beatrix of the Netherlands........Margaret thatcher, Jeff Bezos, George........and of course .Katie.......Romney.....we don't ever want to see your smug

30

face again ....I lived in la costa while they were building your home ....your church. Of the occult. I know I used to be priest in o'side......I grew up........bitch, cunt..........and fuck you Jim of the fbi...I used to work for the fed's to in different situations.......this 16 years of crime will stop.......obviously.....you can't investigate yourself........that is why after the election.......orange jumpsuit time for all that is involved..........and Michele , fuck you you don't like America ....leave bitch.......1972.......looking...what was that movie........after President Trump is elected, there will be a sign , no demons allowed............remember we have the entire list...it is memorized.........I forgot we are stupid and make under 50,000..............we want all misinform abolished ..address the politicians....according to group..........politics, teaching, commerce, world food organization..........they would like to blame it on anything except, what it really is them........they want our guns...........you will have to take them from our cold dead hands..............1/9 c co. scamp 3rd recon.......team.........point...........look in the mirror cracker and repeat after me the C>I>A> are my friends.......sgt. ice rir

June 12, 2016 ·

you in the shit house, you and your cronies started this mess...................we are going to finish it, but not how you think, very carefully...........we are the ones with an significant amount of patience....

Grunt King

June 19, 2016 ·

to all my peeps, and the low heeled spark of high heeled boy's..........on the plains of heaven ......into the dancehalls we go, for a while, picking out clothes, for the evening, with friends, that's how we roll, that's our style, our cars are perfect with that soul Friday glow, into the lights, gleaming, drinks, everywhere, the anticipation of all the girls putting on a show, if you're going to have fun, just join all of us, we hang with the best, it just turns out that way, we have never understood the prejudice, or the underlying fuss, the world is a way of nature and belonging, we want to be part of world, not just on it, we have suffered enough through crisis after crisis, for love ever longing, for everything has been smoke and mirrors, having great moments of our life, not knowing, replacing the conversations, and love with only tears, we have a holy war, we will match them sword for sword, we will send them to their hell, and you can watch them with our Lord.......sgt. ice rir.............to the families and friends of Orlando..........

now that the U.K. is out..................we vote to exit the Muslim brotherhood, c.a.i.r.e, Bilderberg, illuminati, trilateral commission....................cfr, home land security, federal reserve, ...remember , and look up, not required to pay non specie payments.............which means, we owe no one anything, continuing vote, exit from nato, i.r.s, nasa, c.i.a, AmeriCorps, i.r.s. takes our taxes and pays the u.k.......n.a.s.a.is something we have stock in........like have told you many times, they , being jihad insurgents, holy warriors, come as intellectuals, after they achieve political correctness, and establish someone in office, like Barry......Obama........they pass on the responsibility to the next jihad... to make sure Christians become defeated in one con or another....there will be no u.s. of Briton...........this is not Cambodia, or Lebanon, or the Philippines , Malaysia, Indonesia, or the continent of Africa, or the rest of Asia that is now preyed upon by George and the boy's...........We are Americans , and we tried to tell you.........so Barry, why don't you and henry meet up,,,,,,,maybe if you give him some head, maybe he can give you some more advice about being the new, face in a crisis , within the Bilderberg group ....I am sure everyone's waiting for you at the Chicago club...............Hillary's new name..........jihad Hillary................fuck sharia......and fuck all of you that believe in it..........ps...rick Perry of Texas.......you should have been put in front of a firing squad, bush, on agenda 21 in Texas, how many mosques in Texas, Perry.......Bilderberg boy....we are ashamed to have you as a veteran.......you sold your soul ,dickless........good by you cunt of a queen......your next Barry..sgt. ice rir.....

Grunt King

June 24, 2016 ·

and one more thing,...........we want D.C. out of our united
states.................there is no district of Columbia here...........stop the
madness on our constitution, on our intelligence, or the three sided
coin..............go somewhere else with your coins.....like Asia...........I
am sure we have paid off the debts we accumulated during the
revolution, and the civil war...........cut the strings.........lets be
Americans again...........king George died a long time
ago.................sgt. ice rir.

Grunt King

July 2, 2016 ·

hello.........to all my peeps, and the low heeled spark of high heeled
boy's..............where is summer, mom, where did it go, there will be
known summers, child, for this is the end of the show.......you never
see it coming, the mood of the Karmas light, is gone, within a flash
and your limbs are out of sight........the screaming, the crying,
Bilderberg doesn't care, the 1% want their way, and to show
attrition, dominate, using political thugs, and scare......look at the
political history, the political correctness for all to see...........without
it, the Muslim brotherhood said , I could not make you into
me........when you type ,to see capital letters, no more, they have
been replaced by the shadow of the sharia score, to the fathers that
watch from heaven, thinking they had done their military job, only
to watch their families at the hand of the queen, die by her political
mob.........and to the trilateral commission, to whom make money
off our deaths, selling arms to do their bidding......believe me ,
M.U.M...........corps...extracted a lot, I'm not kidding.............we did
our best..........and to my Son and Daughter, I wish you were with us
now, for we are ready, here in the Sierras, Grunt, and the rest of us
will protect you somehow........for we are all Warriors, of past ,
present, and tomorrow,...if you continue down this
path,.....illuminati,....you will meet it with unexpected sorrow......the
billionaires of old, caught up in their bag full of magic, passed on by
their daughters and sons, only to realize, with all of their received
federal reserve, we are the real intellectuals with Guns........this

especially goes out to David Leach....Sr......you need anything..............We will be their Mr. Leach.....jr........Joy.......

Grunt King

July 7, 2016 ·

jimmy, of the F.B.I. , you're an embarrassment to all who served, and still serving...once again the illuminati, trilateral commission prevail.............congress is embarrassing , the fbi is embarrassing Barry Obama the 15 year old that needs his momma is embarrassing.................what's a matter Barry.......internet not working for you.....the media is embarrassing.......knowing are votes don't count , and never did...........embarrassing for us........so jimmy t....................what's in your off shore Bilderberg account say now...come on ...jimmy...give us the balance...you fucking traitor..............there is only one party, and that is the American party.........and of course, the rest of you are fascist socialist pigs.................and your families to.....there will be no more Muslim or communist insurgents allowed.......and after Nov. , all insurgents, including the former president, members of congress, will be investigated for global terrorism, global financial terrorism.......micro management of the state dept. and any other depts. affiliated with the systematic killing of Christians,, and instigating , propaganda, causing upheaval in our Great Nation.................you can take you and your mystery religion and go straight to hell...you may have these young men and women fooled, because YOU TOOK THEIR JOBS AND HANDED THEM A BILL FOR COLLEGE.....................what nationality would you like to live in our America next............Jim.............you friend , the judge......none of us want to hear you name ......you are now on the level of Barry Obama and jihad Hillary...............my article tomorrow from my own account of the fbi.................just getting started Barry...........sgt. ice

Grunt King

July 1, 2016 ·

Loretta, did you really think we were going to let you get away with this.......Loretta, do you plan on killing us, the same way you did in Rwanda............doe's jihad Hillary have the temperament to finish the genocide of Barry the queen ....soothe ..Plan is obvious...are you seriously even thinking about it...............I can just see it...Loretta, Billy, Barry, jihad Hillary, the pope, the queen,...........Saudi royalty, c.f.r., Bilderberg group, trilateral commission, illuminati, and another 132.......laughing their ass off because the media acted like they were surprised by Billy and Loretta.......desperation, produces desperate measures...........please......check out Loretta and Rwanda.....she is a hired thug and traitor sgt.ice rir

Grunt King

July 12, 2016 ·

can you believe that son of a whore, and communist, fascist, tyrant, student of henry k, is speaking in Dallas for something his and his administration are responsible for............the Bilderberg, the illuminati, trilateral commission, CFR...............you are not the new face on Bilderberg,..............you are a little punk that never got schooled, well according to our calculations, your schooling is about to begin. We have been waiting since the summer of 2008..that is how long we have been at the finish line this time, showing desperation, getting sloppy,......a true coward you are, and Our Lord is watching....along with hundreds of millions..........you want to be transparent, don't you Barry...............we won't be looking for any permission to march on a ghetto, called the capital....sgt. ice rir

To Pop's, Pepe' Le Pu...of Michigan............DI BO
CHET.........................remembers Charlie 1/9 U.S. Marines in
jungles far away...............shamus, Sgt. Ice rir.....

Grunt King

and to this day , we will hold our own, for the holy war has long
begun, ...setting aside our true life, and become complacent
before the sun.......when I grow up, I want to be dressed in
blue,........yes daddy when I grow up , I want to be just like

you,.........in elementary school, I knew I had to get strong, in the line of duty, could never get it wrong,......in junior high, I played football, and learned about being a team, and in high school, with the help of the Lord, met the girl of my dreams,. and onto college we went our separate ways, causing many frustrations, and many endless days,.........the summer before the academy, we were happy for a while, I liked the way she had grown, and her style,....through the Academy the physical, spirit, and mind, are tested to the limit, no instructor is kind,.......after graduation, everyone was assigned , I was so happy, I thought I was blind,....onto Dallas, young man, of the Blue, onward, and upward, can't believe it's you,......the girl that you have cared for so long, is joining you in marriage, and will keep you strong,...we had our children, I could only handle three, I told her if she wanted more, I would plant her a tree, the boy's at the office accepted me, I stayed a rookie for about a year, they said it was for my own good, so I would always make it home to the dear,..........the kids were especially lovely this morning, and I kissed my wife goodbye, she looked at me, and said , be careful, with a sigh,......the boy's and I took our positions, the parade was going fine, my first assignment, we could for see no trouble signs,.......after the shooting started, our positions were finally clear, I would carefully move across the street, no time to think of my dear,......as I cleared the pillar's way,............the Lord took me forever, and a day..........Good Bye Love...................the man in Blue.........sgt.ice rir

Grunt King

July 15, 2016 ·

Life during wartime...........demon's, end the parade now, for the veterans in this country, would like to retire, for we arc rctired, takes your mystery religion losses and be gone. You paid yourself, when you were broke. If you wouldn't have used the non-species law.............you would still be broke...cleaning my yard..........yes...the infamous non species payment................Sgt. Ice rir

Grunt King

July 17, 2016

there will be no more sharia law here after the American Party takes over............November...........no more in these United States...Barry...............no one to blame, for the unrest, because, there will be none.......you will be gone...........gone.............all those court dates awaiting you................that's right , Barry, suck o it all the way to the hilt of the queen's sword, Saudi Arabia's.......entities of pathetic royalty...........in 1979 you gave intelligence to the Russian's ...the Intel, where the villages were, you would sell your own grandmother,...............and remember the PPP stands for Humanity.

Grunt King

July 22, 2016 ·

Barry, get off of our TV. , this is not turkey, not yet, because jihad Hillary won't see the shithouse..........remember, Barry, the people, the courts, the Marines, the S.E.A.L.S, all of whom ....let's just say ....jan.21.....................the investigation will have just begun.............Barry the queen...........and remember.....carl Marx..........always blame it on someone else...................and for Mexico ......you will pay for the wall.......................and you will like it..................you sadistic, drug dealing fuck............you remember me from cabo,.......dickless...................you see we know what we're talking about.................................why do you think President Trump, doubled down after the C.I.A briefing............they told him what we, he and the rest of the world knows...............no one will work for her, not the people that matter.............and Mexico, I know you well.......too well.......what was that................gun's being sold to American's and other personnel in beauty shops all over cabo.......while being monitored..........these last 16 years was to make us look bad and everyone else look good.......for an easy take-over,........I guess you we not ready for Grunt and I................as you know we started this Facebook thing in Feb. of 2016..............we have a lot more facts and fact based stories on your way.........this will not continue to be a socialists, demon pig, ran Gov. for the people that made the U.S. possible........by the way, I wouldn't wait

38

for the last minute to start packing for the border. Remember, we have rules in real life. none of them have been used.........lately.............,....but they will be, and I would say, very quickly,.........all for votes, socialist, communist pig votes....................if you have read my posts you'll find , Grunt and I are being kind today........you awoke a crippled old marine, Grunt, my Service Angel,.......and the caregiver..............you realize, you fucked up............all of you responsible for all of the hopelessness, helplessness, greed, will pay a dear price to our Lord, Jesus Christ, Amen...........................sorry about the type o's.......I just sit down to check the ....and well, you know........and to all my new friends...........I was a comedian in my last life, so this is weird...ha-ha............sgt. ice rir.........P.S. chant orange jumpsuits! For jihad Hillary, Barry, the shadow Muslim, Loretta, the Rwanda, genocide lynches...on and on.........

Grunt King

July 27, 2016 ·

To the low-heeled spark of high-heeled boy's, my peeps...the club of Rome...create a crisis; the common enemy of humanity is man. In searching for a new enemy to unite us, we, came up with the idea that pollution, the threat of global warming, water shortages, famine and the like would fit the bill. All these dangers are caused by human intervention, and it is only through changed attitudes and behavior that they can be overcome. the real enemy is humanity itself...............alexander king...club of Rome-premier environmental think tank............consultants to the u.n............."we need to get some broad based support, to capture the public's imagination...so we have to offer up scary scenarios , make simplified, dramatic statements and make little mention of any doubts...each of us has to decide what right balance is between being effective and being honest"...................prof. Stephen Schneider,...Stanford professor of climatology............"we've got to ride this global warming issue. Even if the theory of global warming is wrong-we will be doing the right thing in terms of economic and environmental policy...timothy worth president of the u.n. foundation........" I believe it is appropriate to have an 'over- representation of the facts on how dangerous it is, as a predicate for opening the audience.....al gore...climate change actor........" no matter if the science of global

39

warming is all phony, climate change provides the greatest opportunity to bring about justice and equality in the world.......Christine Stewart former Canadian minister of the environment..........."The data does not matter. We are not basing our recommendations on the data. We're basing them on climate models"...prof. Chris Rolland...Hadley center for climate prediction and research......"the models are convenient fictions that provide something useful...Dr. David frame. Climate modeler, oxford u., I have your modeler dangling sonny..." it does not matter what is true, it only matters what people believe is true..........Paul Wilson...Co-founder-Greenpeace............Sgt. Ice, Grunt...r.i.r.

Grunt King

July 29, 2016 ·

well F.B.I I was hacked again today, when I was delivering a poem to the people, I have been hacked again and again, and I never say the Russia did it, whoever it is, doesn't want to end up in orange jumpsuits......the next time I am hacked, We will go straight to Palo alto, to see the fbi personally, bring my computer, and when Grunt and I start swaying to the beat, and if were not interrupted, well, 1 down,. They know exactly who...and they know that I know........we will try this again......................a poem for Bernie Sanders......there was a time when fate came around to soon, everyone was prepared, but no one knew the gloom, the silent bewilderment, blood leaving the bodies edge, not perceived, and only to feel deceived, where have you gone, oh leader of mine, I have gone back into hiding, using you up and stealing your precious time, you see, I just came out ....for a short while,.......to feed you with propaganda, that's barrack's style,...........as your marching in the streets, the kids are with the grandmas, babysitters, watching and praying their parents will come home in one peace, while Bernie and barrack are drinking scotch, knowing the diversion has worked, seamlessly, and knowing all will cease...................the media has already predicted what you'll do, because they feel you don't want to lose,.......loose what, as everyone is on their way home, gone as they say,.........gone for good,..........this is not the way it was supposed to be,.......on a level playing field, and Bernie and jihad Hillary, maintained their artificial shield,........for many years we have bowed to the Bilderberger group, ...no more we say, for we shall no longer stoop,......it is time to put jihad Hillary's election to rest, for we know are children are the best,............our future here is doubtful and sad, our citizens have no protection, and Bernie, in reality, you and barrack are very glad,.............you see, deception and secret meetings, selling you illusions are part of their profession, and they do it so well, without indiscretion ,........there are two revolutions still moving in the right direction, for liberty, and justice............for all will be are resurrection ....sgt. ice rir.......

Grunt King

August 6, 2016 ·

to Presidential nominee for the American Party..........Donald J. Trump.........request: "War has been declared on Christian's ...As Islamic fundamentalism spreads its tentacles worldwide, it is crucial for the people... to understand the danger, know what to expect, and know what to do about it"- Brigitte Gabriel...................please take her, if she excepts, to all of your town hall meetings, etc..........her performance at the water of life in san Bernardino, she is an Author, and terrorist survivor...........senior pastor, dr. Dan Carroll...............dvd#1088..................she is better live.................she should be assigned a post within the cabinet ....ambassador or anything that say's pay back is a bitch Lebanon...............I have said this to many times.................America is not Lebanon, or the Philippines, continent of Africa, or any other apparent design to subdue Christian's around the world........since Jan. I...grunt king aka sgt. ice have been exploiting the demons........there propaganda will machine will spit out, we're winning all the way to their arrests and demise.......it will happen, in our humble opinion either way......p.s. hey Barry, why don't you go ahead and move a terrorist next to me..............hell, you already did,......john and Susan............bring it on Hillary.......................she has a heart and an address , just like everybody else.............the new address will say Guantanamo bay Cuba..........jihad Hillary is my name for her................

Grunt King

to the low heeled spark of high heeled boy's.........my peeps,
..........subject ; dilemma Youssef,........brazil's president was
suspended amid charges of manipulating government
accounts............end quote....where I come from , that is called
racketeering.......times interview is just like the rest of soro's
media.............first question: how is the fight for impeachment going
?.........answer: non crime......of course I would like to know what a
fucking crime is these day's in Hillary brazil........she believes the
weapon is to fight in a debate, explanation and dialogue...........lie, in
other words...........if she is not found guilty, she wants to reform the
political system ,..Sound familiar, do you believe that the
impeachment is sexist? Misogynistic, in truth. the fact that a woman
became president gives rise to an elevation of women that is very
common, very stereotypical........end quote.........my side.......I.M.F
to Paulo Nigeria Batista jr., new development bank to Paulo
nogueria Batista jr., I.M.F to alexander Antonio tombini, tombini to
dilemma rousseff, I.M.F to Joaquin levy, mossback fonseca panama
papers, to Renan calheiros, to Eduardo cunha, Renan to petro bras,
b.r., and dilemma roussef, what a coincidence uh..Mossback
fonseca, panama papers to Eduardo cunha, to Michel temer, to
dilma rousseff petro bras, b.r. to Guido Manteca, Guido, this is not
fucking risky business, and these are real lives. They do not
care...........anyway, Guido Manteca to Lula da
Silva..........Lula.............., Joaquin levy, continued..., to luau da sila,
and Lula to dilemma.........straight shot,.............I.M.F to Joaquin
levy, to Lula da Silva to dilma rousseff. ....Morgan Stanley,
Citi group, bank of America, to pet bras, br, to you guessed it
.dilemma roussef.........oh yes, one more little demon,...nelson
Barbosa,..................my notes on her are from May, this interview
was on Aug. 8th...........................sgt. ice rir

Hillary is a Bilderberger, they are Nazis, she is also a member of the
trilateral commission, illuminati, and c.f.r.,..........central of foreign
relations,.......educate yourselves black Muslims matter, black
shadow Muslims matter, heathen lives matter, children of the corn
lives matter, pol pot children matter,...........we know the scam, all
too well...nasa,5 doors down, fbi, across the lake,...CIA, down the
road,......why do you think we live in our gated communities, with

our own airports, go ahead and vote for the cunt.............life , as you know it will come down.........it is called attrition,. Ask henry k. chow

August 11, 2016

how is your work out going ?.......you and your family paying cash to journalists.........worldwide......you even have a board for issuing the money, the league of 12..................punk

Grunt King

August 15, 2016 ·

remember, if by some Jesus miracle Donald Trump wins, how many favors is he going to do for you, in Florida.....................in that particular district..............none.......no favors for demons..........you want to play politics, Debbie..........this is politics 101.......be nice.............how old is Debbie, maybe she can't be nice, maybe, she can't wait for the Bilderberger plans to unfold.........if she wins, well..........who are your constituents little Debbie........tell the world what you're getting ready to do to Christians, attrition, agenda 21, the onslaught of the Constitution, and the upholder of the Muslim brotherhood, movement, shadow Muslim movement, shadow party and so on.................elect anyone but her...........she is a traitor,.....................i remember what we used to do for traitors...........

Grunt King

August 16, 2016 ·

destroy evil, you cannot hate, just destroy it................is the military responsible for the leadership in this country at the moment,....yes.....we have lawlessness from top to bottom, but only the military can do anything / some.................look what Barry did to turkey and every other Christian country,........imagine what jihad Hillary will do................Turkey, if you don't want sharia

43

law....Barry finally threatened someone with nato, because it was in the orders interest.........b.l.t.-c.f.r..............every country must be ran by Muslims............my new face could have been perfect, on the Bilderberger ticket.......jihad Hillary exploited me and everyone......................we could have with holder, lynch, jimmy, Billy m., Allen, destroyed Christianity, kill veterans in their homes, Barry signed the law, all they want is federal power over everything..................you want genocide, that is what the Clinton's , and lynch does best, create artificial Intel. That does not exist, and send it out to play...........this is all about artificial power..........they welcome the revolution..........they want the terrorists to get the nukes...they want to be the 1% with their army, not ours, to control all of us at will. This must stop now...Pentagon...as much as you are jaded, we all know ...that's enough, do your job. Start making arrests in the White house and beyond...and in your own dept....................Sgt. Ice r.i.r...Don't tread on me........................

Grunt King

August 30, 2016 ·

john mc Cain is a no good son of a bitch.....we want him out of office, as well as far away from disabled Vets as possible....I have 3 lawyers, you sob just to fight you and your Barry lawyers.....the VA is one thing ....a buffer between you ,and the Pentagon...I mean pentagram..................the VA are lawyers making sure you are part of the genocide.....the doctors, are lawyers.......not literally...trained...for attrition, especially, the ones that are not in compliance. You the patient.....are worm food...no matter how much education you have, military experience, life experience, they will put you down, keep you down, kick you , and then poison you.....I am going to release some of my info tomorrow ...I know how you like facts.....you will be scared to death.......it is from my own records......my lawyers, and family are going to crucify you....va.....get mac Cain out of office, and if his bitch daughter doesn't like Trump.......well...bilder...shut the fuck up....go to Vegas and use those tits for something positive..........

44

Grunt King

August 30, 2016 ·

you see jihad Hillary, genocide Loretta, and Barry the queen want sharia law implemented into our constitution, so we may be the jihadists and not the victim.............and the international police will be used against us, not them, because we won't bow down to sharia law.......you better wake up Hillary, you jihad cunt..........politicians are a dime a dozen, the order does not care what happens to you.......they will just add another face...ask henry Kissinger , if you want to know who the next presidents going to be , which is a joke.............remember , you, your parents, your grandparents etc. votes did not mean a thing.............we know you think you have everything in place......we don't believe things are going to turn out the way you planned. And you, Barry...you cock sucking sob.............the courts will be waiting...Jan 21 all hell breaks out...you know where we live ...we know.................there is no title. Only a heartbeat............you demon ....and jihad Hillary, if you get in........f henry chooses revolution over America taking it's country back.......and for Donald Trump.......stick to your guns......they can kill each other in their own country,.....how many more Muslim takeovers do we have to have, that is generated by our own Gov. the queen, Saudi terrorists.....game over.........you think you have it covered..........#'s to remember..........20,000,000....500,000,000,1.5 trillion..........................sgt. ice rir

Grunt King

August 30, 2016 ·

Jihad Hillary will replace this punk

UN Backs Secret Obama Takeover of Local Police

Obama trickery and treachery knows no limits, as in this deceptive program to draw local law enforcement into the Federal net. Technocracy is predicated on total and centralized control of all key service functions in society.

Grunt King

August 31, 2016 ·

The roots of the Clinton foundation's corruptions can be found in the land stealing policies of Andrew Jackson, the founder of the Democratic Party....library of Congress...............Sgt. Ice rir

Grunt King

August 31, 2016

Democrat john c. Calhoun invented the positive good" school of slavery in which he insisted that slavery was good not only for the master but for the slave. Ever since democrats have been exploiting people while insisting that such exploitation is good for the people being ripped off. Library of Congress.........Sgt. Ice r.i.r

Grunt King

August 31, 2016 ·

I've lived uptown.....I've lived downtown.............I've lived all around.........I've had money, I've had none, I've had money, I've had none,..................but I've never been so broke that i couldn't leave town,.......I'm the changing, watch me change..........the Doors....if the demon gets elected, well........sgt. ice r.i.r......

Grunt King

August 31, 2016 ·

Two things to have at all times: the patriot handbook, and the 10 commandments. and since everyone has their own thing.....a version of the 10 commandments and hope......some people like to keep it scientific, where do they think they got the brain to acknowledge math, an old magic, handed down from universe to universe, you know the chemicals your made of. Believe it or not, you came from the earth. You were not ordered out, like finger hut. everything you see came from this planet if you're missing a few chemicals, they take your blood, and if you need some more earth, they give it to you.....................I am an engineer...plant, and otherwise.....I cannot stand scientists who think they have invented what has already been done to perfection...........and even possible spiritual perfection ....remember: free will/fuck the order.................sgt. ice r.i.r

Grunt King

August 31, 2016 ·

Northern democrat Steven Douglas, who sought to uphold slavery through his doctrine of "popular sovereignty", gives the lie to the idea that slavery battle was between the north and the south- actually it was between the republican and democratic parties. Library of congress. sgt. ice r.i.r.

Grunt King

August 31, 2016 ·

Abraham Lincoln, Americas first republican President, aptly described the difference between the two parties by saying that one thinks slavery is wrong and ought to be restricted, while the other thinks slavery is right and ought to be extended. Library of congress...........Sgt. Ice r.i.r.
Democrat john c. Calhoun invented the positive good" school of slavery in which he insisted that slavery was good not only for the master but for the slave. Ever since democrats have been exploiting people while insisting that such exploitation is good for the people being ripped off. Library of Congress...Sgt. Ice r.i.r

Grunt King

August 31, 2016 ·

1st black President, bill Clinton , whitest president, barrack Hussein Obama, and jihad Hillary...........well, one of the first, in modern times, used her husband's sexploitations as fuel, ...so she could finally be living in emerald city, amongst the others, the order, that is, if she survives them, remember, she with the least amount of money in their order, within their order careers are expendable ......run jihad Hilary, run we say , get elected, run to save your execution stay...............sgt. ice r.i.r.

Grunt King

August 31, 2016 ·

by showing the racists film 'the birth of the nation in the white house, the progressive democrat Woodrow Wilson inspired a Klu Klux Klan revival in the south, Midwest, and west. Wilson also segregated all areas of the federal government, telling black leaders that segregation was for their benefit. copyright by Harris and euing, courtesy of the library of congress........no more games...everyone knows.................I want, we want all media organizations to be present at the next Bilderberger, trilateral commission, illuminati, cfr IMF, royalty...............bash............monsters at the Marriott in one fucking room........imagine.......I know...we know.....your part of the new order...............we now have turkey for a country...........................fuck you Hillary, jihad Hillary.........vote Trump

August 31, 2016 ·

republican crusader Ida b. wells sought to stop the practice of lynching, but she had mixed success because lynching was protected and promoted by democratic party as a technic of keeping blacks down-and preventing them from voting republican. Library of congress...Sgt. Ice r.i.r...Vote Trump

Grunt King

August 31, 2016 ·

republican booker t. Washington, a former slave, inspired the ire of democratic racists when he dined with republican president teddy Roosevelt; democratic senator ben Tillman said, "now that Roosevelt has eaten with that n*gger Washington, we shall have to kill a thousand n*ggers to get them back in there place. " library of congress.......................your so called black leaders no all of this...................they always have...........research ......propaganda must stop..............the people in the streets are not the people visiting the oval office............I have read each group and what they want..............and all I have to say is , who and the hell do you think you are......................vote Trump........sgt. ice rir
progressive Margaret sanger-founder of planned parenthood and heroine to Hillary Clinton-sought to deal with the "unfit" by keeping them out of the country or killing them, her " negro project" was designed to reduce the size of the black penis, I mean population........look, this is serious ...I am scot and Cherokee, Navaho ....we get it.........the scots however: I am I direct descendent of Andrew of Moray of Petty of Scotland. So Hillary, you see, my ancestors did not like you or your husband's family...you understand the history between us...we have dated our family back to 1102...we are natural enemies...Sgt. Ice rir

Grunt King

September 1, 2016 ·

I am listening to AC/DC ....another empty bottle, another empty bed.............I'm going to right on.............right on..........I'm just another empty head,...........get back to the start........another red light night mare........another red light St. one way ticket, going the wrong way..............I'll change my evil ways
....maybe.....................right on looking for a truck.....keep on riding.................have myself a good time............one of these days.....................me I am back in black mother

49

fuckers...........................the Klu Klux Klan was founded in the 1860's and initially focused its terror tactics not on blacks but on white republicans. Library of congress.....................Sgt. Ice rir

Grunt King

September 1. 2016 ·

Night riding and cross burning were two symbols of the KKK. Historian Eric foner calls the clan the domestic terrorist arm of the democratic party, whose main objective was to enforce white supremacy and to keep the South voting monolithically democratic..........library of congress.................tell me, can you look yourself in the mirror.....

Grunt King

September 1. 2016 ·

Hillary Clinton's political technics can be traced back through Saul Alinsky to frank Nitti, # 2 men in the Capone mob...Hillary's America .the film

Grunt King

September 1. 2016 ·

Segregation laws were passed by democrat's legislatures, signed democratic governors, and enforced by democratic mayors, city officials, sheriffs, and vigilante mobs. Segregation was, from the beginning to end, created and sustained by democrats...library of congress..............vote Trump

Grunt King

September 1. 2016 ·

if any claim of progressive fascination with fascism and Nazism seems far-fetched, consider this young JFK toured Germany in the 1930's and praised Hitler as Legend, attributing hostility to the Nazis to jealousy of what they had accomplished...courtesy of the JFK presidential library and museum, Boston

Grunt King

September 1. 2016 ·

Progressive hero franklin Roosevelt cut a deal with a racist democrats in which he agreed, in exchange for their support of his agenda, to block anti-lynching legislation and to exclude blacks from most new deal programs. This shows how progressivism didn't displace racism; rather, it incorporated it. Library of congress...................how much misinformation are you going to feed them for hopelessness.................

Grunt King

September 2. 2016 ·

One of FDR's closest allies was the notorious racist Theodore Bilbo-FDR's choice to run the District of Columbia-who said, "the n*gger would never vote in Washington. hell, if we giv'em the right to vote up there, half the n*ggers in the south will move into Washington and we we'll have a black government." library of congress.............I think it's time for everyone to go to the emerald city and see what's behind the curtain,...........henry Kissinger ....go ahead henry, tell us now, who the next presidents going to be, you sick fuck....you would be the first to be water boarded.................sgt. ice rir

Grunt King

September 2. 2016 ·

originally a member of the southern faction of racists democrats, LBJ saw the civil rights act as a means to keep n*ggers , as he ca this makes me sick. But you must know how it works.............allot of you do ....but I guess when you live a lie long enough........

Grunt King

September 2, 2016 ·

Saul Alinsky- mentor to both Barry Obama and Hillary- was no crusader for social justice; rather, he began his career as a petty street criminal and thief and later learned the art of political intimidation and shakedown at the hands of various Chicago gangs.

Grunt King

September 2, 2016 ·

While young Hillary-at Wellesley College-wrote her thesis on Alinsky, she went beyond Alinsky's outsider shakedown approach to develop her own strategy of shaking down the country from the inside, using the coercive instruments of the federal government...Getty...........................Hillary...........you are a cunt

Grunt King

September 2, 2016 ·

Young Hillary realized what we all know, that bill Clinton is a sex addict, and she saw how she could turn his problem to her lifelong advantage. Hillary's America, the film...........we need a real not pay for play psychiatrist and investigators up in here...you heard about the South American president dilma being impeached

Grunt King

September 2, 2016 ·

Here is the charade of the Clinton marriage on full display; in reality, this is a bargain in which Hillary gets her "pitch man" and in exchange provides protection and cover for bill's predatory sexual behavior. Library of congress...if you vote for this demon. What are you?

Grunt King

September 2, 2016 ·

Just as Evita Peron used her philanthropic foundation to take in 200 million for herself and her husband Juan, Hillary uses the Clinton foundation as a receptacle for hundreds of millions of contributions that are actually bribes in exchange for favors granted through her and bill's political influence. Ass. Press. Getty..........................jihad Hillary....................vote Trump

Grunt King

September 2, 2016 ·

originally a member of the southern faction of racists democrats, LBJ saw the civil rights act as a means to keep n*ggers , as he called them, down on the democratic plantation . Library of congress.................typing this makes me sick. But you must know how it works.............allot of you do ....but I guess when you live a lie long enough...

Grunt King

September 2, 2016 ·

Young Hillary realized what we all know, that bill Clinton is a sex addict, and she saw how she could turn his problem to her lifelong advantage. Hillary's America, the film...........we need a real not pay for play psychiatrist and investigators up in here...you heard about the South American president Dilma being impeached

Grunt King

September 2, 2016 ·

Here is the charade of the Clinton marriage on full display; in reality, this is a bargain in which Hillary gets her "pitch man" and in exchange provides protection and cover for bill's predatory sexual

53

behavior. Library of congress...if you vote for this demon. What are you?

Grunt King

September 2, 2016 ·

Just as Evita Peron used her philanthropic foundation to take in 200 million for herself and her husband Juan, Hillary uses the Clinton foundation as a receptacle for hundreds of millions of contributions that are actually bribes in exchange for favors granted through her and bill's political influence. Ass. Press. Getty...........................jihad Hillary.....................vote Trump

Grunt King

September 2, 2016 ·

terrorists to water board.....off the top of my head.....and i am listening to the Led.............to the low heeled spark of high heeled boy's................and for you Ash, you know my secret...........it shall be a picture moment...............Eduardo cunha, Renan calheiros, Paulo nogueira Batista jr.,Alexandra Antonio tombini, Guido Manteca Michel temer, dilma rousseff, even though she's gone, nelson Barbosa, Lula da Silva, Joaquin levy, George Soros, Barry , bill, Billy, hillary,madame Christine laggard, henry Kissinger, ted Cruz(S.247) which is set up to deport Americans that do not agree with their agenda, not terrorists, we are the terrorists according to them for not wanting to give up our country......we are not going to pay taxes for everyone but us ...fuck you nUK............the list goes on......but you get the picture...........i say all of the Bilderbergers, trilateral, illuminates, cfr personnel, IMF personnel, come out of the closet and explain why they think they should tax us to build their own security, own bank, own army, i don't fucking think so.........1%+10% allowed for monetary and stupidity. They do not worship anything you may know...............the scholars, and probably everyone else knows that by now. imagine , just imagine,......................led zeppelin #3 watch this train roll down the track...............music......bring it on home.....................that's me baby.....you know what I'm saying................................sgt. ice rir

Grunt King

September 3, 2016 ·

Jihad Hillary's Pharma will replace them, so we can die quicker...isn't that right, you demon

Statement by National Security Council Spokesperson Ned Price on U.S.-China Enhanced Control Measures for Fentanyl

Grunt King

September 3, 2016 ·

Articles: How the Clintons Gave American Foreign Policy its Muslim Tilt

The Clinton role in the rise of Islamic irredentism has now come full circle. Bill Clinton might get the credit for the original Muslim tilt. Bosnia (1992-95) set the table for a series of interventions that gave birth to the so-called Arab Spring and any subsequent triumphs of Islam fascism. Irony...

Grunt King

September 8, 2016 ·

Collin Powell is a liar. Nothing is to be sent unsecured. Nothing. Bush is a liar. Clinton is a liar. CIA has all e-mails, all the e-mails were sent from somewhere, and that somewhere has a copy, everyone knows the rouge Bilderbergers.................barely age 19..in charge of CIC and JIC 12 hours a day, and that ain't nothing.......I am almost 60 now..............stop lying, stop embarrassing yourself...........this is a lawless presidency, and no one will be arrested until Jan 2017.....we might even include the bush's...........so long jihad Hillary so long....sgt. ice rir

Grunt King

September 11, 2016 ·

We all find it a little strange that the US government has the authority to take your passport if you owe money to the IRS. President SOB slid it in with the highway bill, Dec. 2015. You like that...the little fuck setting everything up for jihad Hillary. Now peewee Cruz, senator that is...whatever that means, introduced a bill that would revoke the citizenship of any American providing material assistance. What do you think the pentagon, gram doing? the Bilderbergers, trilateral commission, illuminati, IMF.......and lets nothing is done in secretion forget the CFR........they are the global terrorists in every fashion........watch what happens to the stock when Barry Sotoro leaves..........kicking whites out. letting the Asians, southeast Asians, blacks Mexicans. anyone they prefer over whites and middle class......the BLTCFR wants us eliminated............in other words, it's crunch time. To some people taking some ones citizenship is a time- honored way of dealing with political enemies. In ancient Rome you could lose your citizenship for theft, murder, or treason..................every swinging dick from the president on down should be tried for treason. I know. I used to be in intel.G-2..............once you lose your status in Rome. the hit man cometh..............in 1935 if you were not German. you lost your citizenship. Simple...any one dark skinned became subjects of the state. They changed their constitutional law to kill the Russian and polish Jews...the UK can't get enough of this law...in 2006 they passed a little that said "deprivation is conductive to the public good"..............very these deliberations are done in secrecy. The UK has stripped many people of their citizenship...natural born included. Two have been killed in drone strikes, one secretly deported to the US. .....Americans could lose their citizenship in a state dept. meeting. No trial...they want them in - us out...Canada has joined the march. Now with the Cruz Expatriate Terrorist Act. (S.247), the little fuck has set everything up for jihad Hillary..........or at the time himself..........there was a little guy called cantor ...when he went, well you know and a little guy in congress that miss spoke about jihad Hillary, the committee, her poles all in the same breath ......you didn't think we missed that. Jihad Hillary and Putin are in the same group..............everyone knows......Bilderbergers......you can appeal the state depts. decision....to no avail. Charge: material assistance...could you be guilty? The Cruz proposal does not define it. really....the Terrorist Material Support Statute, forbids providing "material support" to anyone engaged in an offense identified as a federal crime of terrorism.......wow, ok what is that? by merely giving advice on how to peacefully resolving disputes..............now do you understand why the war was started 15 years ago, and even before that...they don't want it to end ......the biggest money maker......attrition.......in any way . let's face it revoking citizenship is a lot of power....then they can murder you ......you know like the law Barry signed to kill marines and soldiers door to door for being disgruntled ..You mean intelligent. the global trend is clear. if jihad Hillary is allowed in our White-House she will use these laws against us, not them...if she is elected, we will become the political enemies of the US......get a second nationality and passport just in case..............to my

56

peeps and the low heeled spark of high heeled boy's...................and
Presidential nominee Donald Trump-VOTE TRUMP......sgt. ice. RIR

Grunt King

September 14, 2016 ·

to the environmentalist: animals do nothing to you, yet you kill them easily
because they can't talk and kill us because we can./ SGT. ICE RIR PS no matter
how many different Heavens there are, Barry , barrack will not be accepted.
........and the Jews don't want jihad Hillary to destroy their future,.......even
though they pretend to

Grunt King

October 4, 2016 ·

To the three personnel who used to be on the other end of 703-671-9810.................you were right, the Jackal was not a political consultant............................SGT. ICE RIR Grunt King

October 1, 2016

It was a great day to be close to God

06.10.2016 00:02

Napoleon pointed out "Terrorism", War, and Bankruptcy are caused by the privatization of money, issued as a debt, and compounded by interest "-......so where does it all start......... the Grasberg mine 1.9 miles from grass mountain ...and the Hertzberg mine.....main office : Arizona...president : George mealy, geologist , :Forbes Wilson. Owner : god Frey Rockefeller....Robert Lovett........financed by Freeport Sculpture..............................Grasberg mine location : Papua province , Indonesia...coordinates : 4 d-310 d, 137 d, 6 d, 57 d. production :610, 800 tons of copper.......58,474,392 grams of gold , 74,458,971 grams 0f silver per financial report..Co. Freeport mc Moran. Freeport sold 13 % interest sale of interest for 1 billion in cash.................centralization of credit in the hands of the state, by means of a national bank with state capital and an exclusive monopoly. The communist manifesto. in the case of the Bolshevik revolution-or any other-I am the bank- therefore : lip service is a convenience ....Mr. Rockefeller....des..........I have quoted rocky saying this a few times in my posts....so today..........as yesterday....when can we look forward to tomorrow...the long run...................jihad Hillary has not sued or will sue over the movie or the book Hillary's America......why.....because it's true.........look : Hillary Clinton is a Bilderberger, part of the trilateral commission, illuminati, IMF, a dark portal into everything that is mad and dark. she will establish chaos , genocide, pharm , Monsanto attrition, the unleashing of the Muslim brotherhood again, listening to CAIRES bullshit, our children watching beheadings, burnings, rape pillage....it will come straight to you if jihad Hillary is elected. That's how serious it is. There will be justices appointed......sharia law will be implemented, 2nd amendment extracted, Christians will be eradicated, and in our own country, no less. you see we have become extinct...you just don't know it yet......we are a 3rd world............the CIA< FBI are treating us as if we were the enemy...............for a long time now we have been playing into the enemies hands : the Bilderbergers. Remember the Gambino's, Colombo's, Bonannos, the Genovese's and the Luccheses. Today they have been replaced by US, china, Japan, Europe and the IMF........international monetary fund.......NON_SPECIES_PAYMENT. Wait until jihad Hillary unleashes the UN urban peace-keeping force, AMERICORE.....there weapons are electronically fixed to them...codes....she will do everything to systematically start a revolution......if the police do not agree .....who knows...if ICE does not agree, who knows, if the border patrol disagrees , who knows.........if some of the military............who knows......we are lawless.........and British courts don't apply to us anyway.........this is America, our name is not in all caps. We may get help from our own men and women in uniform ...but a lot of the younger crowd are brainwashed just like the pol-pot in 75-79.....look him up.....he is just like barrack o.......or Barry the queen...........our country is for sale.......in a meeting with the Chinese Barry -o told the Chinese to take what we owed them in land........speaking of that , Barry will be down to 12 soon......and you're not getting a fucking raise looser......no-class-cracker.......with a no class demon coming in right behind you..........for you women voting for Jihad Hillary, I hope you like sex, because the holy warriors do, you like watching rape up close and not on the internet. someone at your door arresting you for being you.........Christians exterminated in front of you, heads removed on a regular basis, women and children buried and burned alive.............everything you have seen from a distance will come to your door step just like Lebanon 1982........the CIA sets all these countries up to be taken over by Muslim insurgents..............remember what -Brigitte Gabriel said :war has been declared on Christians...as Islamic fundamentalism spreads its tentacles worldwide, it is crucial for the people.....to understand the danger, know what to expect, and know what to do about it ....Talismanicloldols.org.........the devils horseman, the rest of the story, shooting the sacred cows of money, generation zero, America, Hillary's America, taking chance, and of course ....boys of co. c.................just a couple of things you may like..............sgt. ice rir.............Grunt King.

Grunt King

October 15, 2016 ·

'Send us your ambassadors; and thus we shall judge whether you wish to be at peace with us or at war...if you make war on us, the Everlasting God, who makes easy what was difficult and makes near what was far, knows that we know what our power is'............................From a letter by Mangku Khan to King Louis IX of France, 1254................Sgt. Ice RIR.............MUM

60

CORPS..........................1/9 -SCAMP-G-2.................can I get a
ooh-ra, can I get a ooh-ya................if everything goes wrong on

I believe Donald Trump is showing the United States, what happens when someone who is NOT controlled by politics, cannot be bought, and frankly, is "just an American". Just what happens. Democrats hate him, Republicans can't control him, and the government wants to destroy him. So, if no party backs him. Most likely, he is a threat to their agendas. Which in turn, means he is a threat to thier lies and deceptions. It probably means he is exactly what America needs right now. People are always saying, we need to get every career politician out of politics, might as well start at the top.

If no party likes you, your probably doing it right

Nov. 9 I wouldn't want to be communist insurgent or a Muslim insurgent in this 3rd world shithole Nov. 9 I wouldn't want to be communist insurgent or a Muslim insurgent in this 3rd world shithole..

To Presidential American Party: Donald Trump, to my peeps and the low heeled spark of the high heeled boy's ATTENTION MRS.HILLARY RODEM CLINTON: Henry Kissinger: and especially for Elaine Knust, CIA assassin, former high priestess of Indiana. and of course Lucifer, the Romanian hacker who refused to work for the CIA, NSA, embarrassed Colin Powel, Dorothy Bush Diane, Sidney L. , Hillary Clinton, international markets, shadow party and the illuminati...............pam Shaffer received a report from Pensacola Fl. date : 9/19/01, time 11;43..fema officials told the pastor that under martial law we've decided to seize your church and use it for a base ops.do they have the power ?yes, under martial law, fema can seize home, separate family, your vehicles, supplies, church and more....what boy wonder glen needs his ass kicked beck wants...........you see, executive order out guns the constitution.........they like that. Executive orders will turn America into a police state and military dictatorship, Christians and other groups the right to assemble will be impossible. He or she can evoke all emergency powers...and then they shall they deliver you up to tribulation and put to death. No rapture came to rescue Sudanese Christians from Muslim persecution and literal crucifixion in many cases. No rapture saved the Cuban Christians who died with Jesus Christ on their lips in front of Castro's death squads ..."but he that Endured to the End shall be saved-not he that shall be raptured Matthew : 24 one young pastor in southern Ca. said this was a premonition of a holocaust. Michael Maholy, 20 yeas naval Intel/CIA and previously a dedicated worker for the NWO under bush sr. Mike blew the whistle and decided to blow the whistle on the entire NWO agenda.we120, 000 of modern guillotines manufactured in japan and china are here. The boxcars with shackles are here......look it up...I didn't need to. ----if you young ones think you're exempted for worshiping Satan think again. This is about attrition....America needs to be down to 20 mil and the world 500 million....this is a holy war, us against them...whoever they may be.....Hillary. We Satanists in the CIA hate the Christians because they are one thing that stands in the way of our implementing the NWO...so we came up with the concentration camps. Of course there being investigated......right. even helped draw up some of the blueprints for some of them, although I greatly regret my role now, never the less, they stand to this day and will be activated under martial law......we lusted for the hour of martial law when we could finally get are hands on them legally......I tell you it will be brutal rape, torture and death for them once arrested and taken to the concentration camps under martial laws. The boxcars and shackles are in place across America to haul resisters away. Nazi style, Bilderberger style.FEMA ordered 120,000boxcars with shackles. FEMA is working with the UN ordering guillotines and

63

body bags. You wonder why there constructing tracks 200 miles from nowhere. the prisoner cars are too high and too wide for our tracks and overpasses....remember 1944 Harvard mark ibm computer.......in the mid 1990's there was a party at the Dunklin Memorial Camp in Okeechobee Fl. Chark Lakin of Archways Institute , a listening party on research regarding Satanism in America today. Several lecturers were invited including former CIA assassin who also was formerly powerful high priestess over a large region of America. She is now a Christian. Following a series of lectures, we left the facility and there was another get together at the former assassins home. When we arrived, she began to unexplainably cry. I asked her what was wrong. She said with tears and replied -do you think God could ever forgive me. For what? We killed Keith Green. We Satanists held a tribunal in America and determined that he must die. He was drawing more young people than the government. It is that simple. I even know how. The technique the CIA used its rights to inspect the plane by night, and to ensure it would go down. There would be no evidence found. We are trained to employ such techniques...many assassins in the CIA are Satanists and have no problem killing. The reason I changed to Christianity was because right before their death, during the ritual, they would smile. .she became a Christian because she felt God was Stronger. Admission of former CIA assassin and Satanist high Priestess, now a Christian lecturer / author / and exposing the NWO and Satanism. The antichrist NWO is replacing communism with a new brand of Gnosticism identified as pantheist- environmentalism ....this religion worships mother earth and its members are Satanists who proudly slander Jesus Messiah and Christian sexual morals. the pope is no more than pope as I am it is a co. people that believe in a higher positive power and positive energy for every one ...that is what I believe in......Sgt. Ice RIR.....Grunt King......1/9 scamp g-2 etc. don't fuck with us Henry..Think NWA not NWO and that's an order Henry....you know who I AM

Grunt King

October 21, 2016 ·

Loretta lynch is a no good satanic cunt: no one in Groveland likes you. Not one retired official up here likes you and do you know how many of us are here....................you Rwanda genocide demon. did you order the body bags, the box cars with shackles, 120,000 modern guillotines just for us Catholics, Christians, anyone that doesn't agree with you ....you fucking Bilderberger demon........you illuminati whore. President Trump is going to put you in shackles and torture you ...you fucking sadistic no good waste of flesh........look it up ..Sgt.Ice RIR Grunt King...

Grunt King

October 23, 2016 ·

Fuck you illuminati ....Sgt. Ice RIR
When there is beauty there is peace.................making America Great again.....?

Grunt King

October 24, 2016 ·

Look, it is so simple. if the government is lawless and the commanding general, chief of staff will not engage in along with federal marshals in arresting Barak Hussein Obama, Loretta Lynch, James Toomey, Elijah Cummings and all the communists, fascist, Satanists, Bilderbergers, trilateral commission, illuminati, media, you why? Your surrounded...............there is no such thing as parties. There is them 11% and us. I say we win

Grunt King

October 26, 2016 ·

You are not from Chicago. My family is from Chicago. You are from underneath henry Kissinger's desk. You went to school in Indonesia. You sat at a desk where a Christian used to sit. They had been slaughtered. You listen to the clerics, as the screams of the children's make you comfortable and safe.........Sgt. Ice.....RIR

Grunt King

October 26, 2016 ·

There are only 6 parties. The American Party, Bilderberger, trilateral commission, CFR-sister to Bilderbergers, IMF, Jihad Hillary's fav. And the illuminati. remember when jeb took all your trees..............that will be child's play compared to the illegals your about to receive again...............fuck you and your Jihad brother.............if Mr. Trump and Mrs. Trump............obtain the white house the whole family is going to jail-Dana....remember 9/11 monies have to be paid back ....the Arabs will spill their guts..........but I am sure they went down in that Egypt flight........CNN really covered that..................you are just one big Hollywood Sgt. Ice RIR..........

Grunt King

October 29, 2016 ·

hey Joe Biden ....you know and we know the FBI cannot release any information during an on-going investigation...............what a rouge..................Sgt. Ice RIR..............and suck my marine dick ....you fucking Traitor.....................I talk to royalty almost every day........Thailand wants you gone...........away...........no one wants Jihad Hillary...........Priestess illuminatus.........we don't need demon attritions

Grunt King

October 28, 2016 ·

there is no requirement to send a letter to Congress announcing yet another investigation.........James, James,..............was it Barry soetoro's, Loretta genocide lynch, jihad Hillary.........or is henry saying,......how are we ever going to them to trust Michelle ....soetoro the face no one even knows.....................it is a rouge...............Talismanicldols.org

Grunt King

October 29, 2016 ·

to Presidential American nominee, Mr. Donald J. Trump ,Wife and fam..........off the cuff...........the ones that are crying , the spirits you can't see..........coming up from the ground to join the battle to be........the is confusion amongst the young.......who to trust and when to run............because there getting paid to think..........and we're getting paid to sink.........the manipulation of realism mis-information and the facts...........they are groomed from youth to never attack........all but you may, you may if we approve and then we have you for us , transformation is smooth...........when they send you off they don't expect you to come back, the Bilderbergers are laughing while they count their money by the stack..........anything for attrition, kill'em by the millions, may the Christians rot in their tomb........their conflicts are predicted in advance, the mother doesn't know her child's dead when she or he leaves the womb........everything has been concluded , they have excepted the sign to destroy all of us while they drink their wine........remember, we are many , they are few...........we are the marines and soldiers who live our life true.........we have come out of the ground to serve our God and you...........Sgt. Ice RIR..............Talismanicldol.orgs samlakkhana phonthep..................

Grunt King

October 30. 2016 ·

Do you know why 1/9 wore ears around their necks? heads were too cumbersome...........personally Grunt and I like the Columbian necktie................don't you love Nicaragua by way of costa Rica...........just think MUM CORPS........................Mr. Peterson would have loved you...................Satanist................Sgt. Ice 1/9, g-2 scamp, pt.mugu, d-3rd recon, d-t-JIC CIC.......go ahead George ...ask me anything....punk.........................remember I get to do the water-boarding........" To be prepared for war is one of the most effective ways of preserving peace" George Washington-1st American President...........

Grunt King

October 31, 2016 ·

"Do not go where the path may lead, go instead where there is no path and leave a trail"-Ralph Waldo Emerson....

Grunt King

October 31, 2016 ·

Mr. FBI director. There will be no sympathy vote. She is not the victim you shameless SOB.......Presidential American Party nominee, Donald J. Trump may feel sorry for your lame ass, but I know how you operate..............and don't worry about what you think you know, that's why I have lawyers fighting your arrogant pompous asses. She should have been already in jail. Prison. PUT UP OR SHUT THE FUCK UP YOU FUCKING LOW_LIFE..........and fuck you Barry...........soetoro ....you fucking crack-head.............and for you jihad Hillary.. ...and Michelle...........................Guantanamo for all of you...including Comey.............................and everyone who knew..........make someone do their job.................I can't wait to see the look on your faces when my case comes up Bilderbergers.............Sgt. Ice RIR

Grunt King

November 2, 2016 ·

Grunt King

August 30, 2016 ·

you see jihad Hillary, genocide Loretta, and Barry the queen want sharia law implemented into our constitution, so we may be the jihadists and not the victim.............and the international police will be used against us, not them, because we won't bow down to sharia law.......you better wake up Hillary, you jihad cunt...........politicians are a dime a dozen, the order does not care what happens to you.......they will just add another face...ask henry Kissinger , if you want to know who the next presidents going to be , which is a joke.............remember , you, your parents, your grandparents etc. votes did not mean a thing.............we know you think you have everything in place......we don't believe things are going to turn out the way you planned. And you, Barry...you cock sucking sob.............the courts will be waiting.......Jan 21 all hell breaks out....you know where we live ....we know.................there is no title. Only a heartbeat............you demon ....and jihad Hillary, if you get in........f henry chooses revolution over America taking it's country back.......and for

70

Donald Trump.......stick to your guns......they can kill each other in their own country......how many more Muslim takeovers do we have to have, that is generated by our own Gov. the queen, Saudi terrorists.....game over.........you think you have it covered..........#'s to remember..........20,000,000....500,000,000,1.5 trillion...........................sgt. ice rir

Grunt King

The FBI-FACEBOOK HAS SHUT ME DOWN_ NOT ALLOWING ME TO SEND OR WRITE ANYTHING POLITICALLY_ I WOULD NOT HAVE TO HAVE DONE THIS_IF OUR LIVES WERE NOT IN SERIOUS DANGER. they will not allow me to share, post any of my political posts any past writings poems.....the crackers running scared....jihad Hillary's running scared --run "CHARLIE" run......I have been on the phone with Nigeria , India, so called Facebook-managers ....all part of the rouge . I have a civil rights attorney that will be taking care of Hillary, Barry the drag-queen, you voted for him.........Facebook, and 2 lawyers taking care of the VA......and 1 real-estate lawyer for sustainable development......make sure you have plenty of lawyers......remember: there is no such thing as parties or voting........or at least . And to the Bilderbergers and Facebook, their sister the CFR trilateral commission......and illuminati...the IMF......the only nation that will benefit truly are the Muslims......you put a low life crack head in the highest office. Why...because he is weak.... he sucked cock his entire life to get where it is. Michelle I wouldn't let her walk my dog.....jihad Hillary, pervert bill in the shithouse...mac-daddy Barry soetoro, pervert.......which makes her a pervert......................weak leaders, strong CIA. STRONG MORMON FBI.......strong people weak government makes weak people strong Bilderberger's, etc. they have addresses and phone #s just like we do .....Everything is on my posts.....when they shut me down the Thursday night for the DNC.....I knew it ....just a matter of time................and for the decision about voting fraud.......that's what bino's and night goggles are for .make sure you have an attorney present....and always travel in separated groups to mobilize to one sector. You see there has been a horrible thing called fascism, and right now that is the state of our country. Take it back just take it back...........Sgt. Ice

RIR.....PS and for the Sunni on FOX builder. ....fuck you. You can use your computer easily, can't you........? you arrogant bitch you said no one will vote according to the report or basis of a political zeitgeist...........esoteric agenda..............Samlakkhana phonthepTalismanicIdol.org ....Sgt. ICE........Grunt King.....

Grunt King

November 2. 2016 ·

Just for the record. Barry soetoro may pardon everyone but he cannot pardon himself...................you're going to Guantanamo crack-head........and you being the mac-daddy ha ha........you will sing like a canary and everyone will go down. Can't share any posts so I'm writing........remember, maintain the middle class. Maintain our constitution so there will be no sharia law. Key issue: no sharia law. PERIOD............this is not LEBANON!...........1982 look up how the Muslims just slipped in. ....all preplanned by their administration and the insurgents. you see , the Muslims come in through the political structure.....they are full on macs....then the administration ran actually by the illuminati send in the troops under martial law. Lebanon was a democracy.....looks how many democracies have been lost in 8 years. And you never know who the troops are.

Grunt King

November 26, 2016 ·

now this, this is a story that should have made it to Hollywood.............but Disney said no..........I was there to make a deal.........she ,.....being like us..........and every worker Asian, said they didn't except outsiders, even though we were invited just to save protocol............me

Grunt King

November 28, 2016 ·

You're a FRAUD
Will Obama leave office in 2017?

Question: Why are Americans so certain there will be a presidential election in 2016 and that Barack Obama will leave office in January 2017? Answer: Because it's the law and because it's American tradition. However, we currently have a man in the White...

Grunt King

December 25, 2016 ·

Stay educated.............
252 Examples of Obama's Lies, Law-breaking & Corruption

The dirty dealings of the White House.

Grunt King

December 25, 2016 ·

Stay educated..........
- 50 Things Barack Obama Has Done Wrong

Why would anyone dislike Barack Obama? Could it be because of what he's done in the White House? As you get a refresher on the national nightmare that has been Barack Obama's presidency, keep in mind that the biggest difficulty in compiling it...

Grunt King

December 25, 2016 ·

Militants..............artificial............to weak

37 Statistics Which Show How Four Years of Obama Have Wrecked the U.S. Economy

The first four years of Obama were an absolute train wreck for the U.S. economy.

Grunt King

December 25, 2016 ·

An errand boy, sent by grocery clerks to collect a bill..................and we stuck it right up your ass.........

10 Ways Obama Has Failed as President

We are so over with being impressed by this president.

Grunt King

December 25, 2016 ·

What a child.....poor Barry

75

BREAKING: Army General Exposes Barack Obama in a BIG WAY After Resigning - The Political Insider

Outgoing Army Chief of Staff General Ray Odierno just dropped a bombshell on the American people. This top Army general admitted during an interview exactly what…

Grunt King

December 25, 2016 ·

5 Things President Obama Has Done to Destroy America

People have cause to either rejoice or mourn depending on whether their governing authorities are God-fearing or unrighteous.

Grunt King

December 25, 2016 ·

22 Navy SEALs among 30 U.S. troops killed in Afghanistan as NATO helicopter is shot down

U.S. officials confirm that the dead included 22 SEALs from the elite SEAL Team 6 unit that carried out the mission to kill Osama bin Laden.

Grunt King

December 26, 2016 ·

Some people don't know their oppressed until it's over................

Grunt King

January 9 ·

Grunt King *to* Judge Jeanine Pirro

April 22, 2016 ·

I love you all, all my peep's from all over the world. I want to send love out to boy's from Benton park to Gravois 44 to Maryville back when I used to think back and click clack....from St. Louis...........Dear entity of Saudi Arabia.....Ambassador Sheikh gave Basnan 73,000$ for Prince Bandar to pay for his wife's . Princess Haifa Faisal to have a thyroid operation. The money was given to Majeda Dweikat. Al-Bayoumi, Khalid, Alewat, the hijackers met at a restaurant in San Diego .The funds of 73,000$ was released to Al Bayomi after the meeting with the other two. The visa for Al -Bayoumi was extended by Ambassador Sheikh on the same day. Background on Al-Bayoumi: year 2000-Saudi Gov. civil aviation, defense dept.Basnan returned to Saudi Arabia, Dweikat deported to Jordon. The windshield cowboy said job well done. It would have taken years, if ever for this to happen. To start the beginning of a 3rd world war. Shame on you Do you remember flight 800. Bill Clinton had a missile launched from a sub, destroying the plane - who was on that manifest? There were hundreds of witnesses; the FBI called them all a liar. All the same, probably Hillary's idea...I wish they would not capitalize her name. The white house and I do mean it's the whitest it's ever been, unfortunately have housed many terrorists over the years by their own description. I have a t -shirt that say's been fighting terrorists since 1492, being truly part Indian. I felt it appropriate. Do you wonder why no one wanted jeb bush to run, let alone win ....we like is Kennedy Center. During the bush administration the democrats, headed by Mr. Schumer wanted the letters opened. Sen. Sam Brownback R. of Kansas voted against it. Now the Republicans want the letters, and Barry is against it. What a shock.........he has been to Saudi Arabia more than any other president. It is called world domination. I forgive American trained guerillas for doing what they do. who trains guerillas by the dozens . sends them off to kill their cousins . the CIA man , the fucking CIA man....Who can take sugar from a sack , fill it with LSD and put it back , the CIA man ,fucking CIA man.....Who had a meeting with God took his staff , then took his Rod , the CIA man , the fucking CIA man.......my pts. Shakes, and baby seizures, sweating have taken over.....With the new law here they can storm the house shoot my service dog, my caregiver and me. Washington is one of the largest terrorist organizations in the world.................time to go back to the Jungle. ....Take it away families.............Sgt. Ice rir

Grunt King shared his post.

January 9 ·

Grunt King *to* **Judge Jeanine Pirro**

April 14, 2016 ·

Your comments are great. People need to read the book Shadow party and need to go after EPA for allowing Oil companies polluting our ground water a lobbyist to Hillary and Monsanto killing us through GMO killing the bees and ecosystem killing our food and making people very sick. Cruz is bought and paid for by Monsanto. Should we the people copy Thailand?? We need establishment to take us the citizen seriously. If they kill us who is buying consuming any products??? Robots need just a handful people for maintenance and they are not consumers what are they thinking only short terms as always. Look what they have done to the world. Shame on them.

Grunt King

January 10 ·

One Last Treasonous Act=> Obama Approves Uranium Shipment to Iran - Enough to Build 10 Nuclear Weapons

WOW! How Much More Damage Will Obama Inflict on the World Before he Leaves Office? Apparently Barack Obama wasn't satisfied...

Grunt King

January 10 ·

I really wouldn't push it........fascists ...I really wouldn't Sgt. Ice rir

Grunt King

January 18 ·

I guess the communists aren't coming on the20th. The Bilderbergers, the sister CFR, IMF, Trilateral commission, looks like a few of the illuminati will make it. Hey know to keep their enemies close. I guess the rest of them will be in Switzerland plotting to overthrow President Donald J. Trump..

West: 80 communists in the House

Says he's "heard" many Democrats are members.

Grunt King

January 18 ·

we can stand on our own......if someone needs help.........especially Christians....non - communists or jihad.......this is a holy war.......and yet he let the out anyway.......Barry: you're the son of a communist hor....I didn't realize 1/2 the US was commie ....but when I did , we stopped it. Remember me Barry: Mckinleyville ca. 2008

The founding of NATO: What is it really? -- Sott.net

When NATO was founded, that was done in the broader context of the US Marshall Plan, and the entire US operation to unify the developed Atlantic countries of North America and Europe, for a coming Cold War allegedly against communism, but...

Grunt King

January 18 ·

If we have to, we will take off our suits and put on our camies, Girl Scout, militant, gangsters....hey Barry. You're upset because your communist party lost

Democrats BOMB Republican HQ in Orange County, North Carolina - The Geller Report

Facebook Twitter Google+ Governor Pat McCrory called the weekend firebombing of a North Carolina Republican headquarters "an attack on our democracy." What...

Grunt King

January 18 ·
·

A communist

Rep. John Lewis Owes the Country an Apology for His Racist Insults at Godless Convention

Outrageous. Rep. John Lewis (D-GA) a civil rights legend, who lied about being called an n*gger by tea...

Grunt King

January 18 ·

Fuck you, you commie low life- do you know how many jumpsuits you will need for your pathetic administration................orange

Ex-Black Panther: 'John Lewis is an illegitimate congressman'

Former Black Panther Mason Weaver says U.S. Rep. John Lewis is a "civil-rights turncoat" who turned on his people and has "presided over the destruction of black...

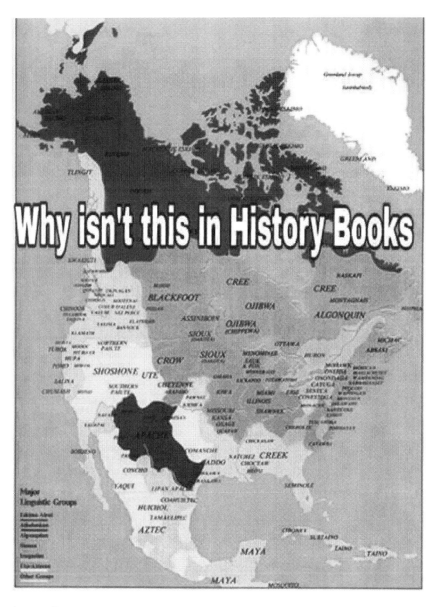

Comment yes and share if you agree that Native American history should be taught properly in schools.

#NativeAmericanRights

Grunt King

January 23 ·

Treason, George......you and the entire administration.......Sgt. Ice reconnaissance intelligence Report

Report: Billionaire George Soros Had Ties to 50 'Partners' of the Anti-Trump Women's March on Washington

News Report: Billionaire George Soros Had Ties to 50 'Partners' of the Anti-Trump Women's March on Washington Published January 23, 2017 Facebook0 Twitter0...

Grunt King

January 23 ·

USO

January 23 ·

This is hard to hear: nearly 90% of our service members say the general public doesn't truly understand the sacrifices they and their families make every day, a...

Add your name: Send gratitude to our service members

Help the USO reach 50,000 messages of gratitude sent to our men and women in uniform by the end of the month as part of our Campaign to Connect.

Grunt King

We are an established country. I helped make it that way....the laws have not been followed for 8 years. And now that they are, you're up in arms. Well, I will tell you this, we will let you embarrass yourself a while longer and then..........just like the election surprised you.....we will surprise you.......you see, that is why Loretta the genocide lynch is in Chicago. she must start deepening the sewer somewhere....since Washington fired her....demon whore, worked for a son of a communist whore....who worked for Soros's, who worked for himself and the CFR<IMF< builders, trilateral, etc. there all little punks with money.......they have brainwashed you to hate your own country. The name...hated their own country....gulf...loved the country......Iraq. Hated their

83

country........afghan......these politicians have played you right into your unsafe artificial world. You are more unsafe than you have ever been because of the establishment....not the pretend parties....the repubs. caught on right away....another words, they finally caught up with President Trump and the rest of us...s , ray, Nancy, veronica, and myself new exactly what he was, been groomed for, his declaration of war on these united states. The only thing he committed was treason on many levels........his admin. must pay........so if any of you non - law abiding illegals or assholes " miss-informed want to come up to Groveland , mariposa, midpines, Columbia, Sonora, etc. to spread your 80 IQ go ahead...we'll be here........my dead friends from the marine corps and civil service say....FUCK YOU_---GROW - UP maybe there will be a draft, you can use that college education.......you don't even qualify...who would want you......GET OUT COMMIES, FACSISTS...SGT. ICE RIR

Grunt King

January 29 ·

How does it feel?
Five killed in Quebec City mosque shooting: mosque president

Five people were killed after gunmen opened fire in a Quebec City mosque during evening prayers, the mosque's president told reporters on Sunday.

January 30 ·

We are in charge, not you. We the People..............you cunt of Barry's and Loretta the genocide lynch......................you better wake up........HELLS ON THE WAY.......payback is a bitch.............uh Soros...................

Trump fires acting U.S. attorney general after she refuses to enforce immigration order

84

U.S. President Donald Trump on Monday fired acting U.S. Attorney General
Sally Yates after she ordered Justice Department lawyers not to enforce
Trump's...

Grunt King

January 31 ·

For you fascists....there will be no sharia law implemented in these United States

Grunt King

January 31 ·

I would advise the Soros media to be very careful.....the head of
snake: chop chop

Grunt King

January 31 ·

Democratic politics.....looks real-not real-demons don't care about
anyone except other demons

Grunt King

February 11 ·

to the low heeled spark of the high heeled boy's, and my daughter
Jenny......once upon a time in a land of love and true
emotion....there was the collective, only for love and
devotion....times were eventful, all the souls sored, only for the
collective to get bored...it embraced itself to tightly, and the rules
became unsound....it was the politics of the devil making his first
round......divide and conquer, our favorite ploy,......only to act like
it's never been used, but it still brings you joy....the ground is filled

85

with warriors from all walks of life, the political , theocracies stalling and causing human strife......they come and they go with only one thing in mind, to kill all Christians, who have been so kind.....who are these holy warriors, Satanists, and scientology.....illiterates....their fraction from the collective is quite in-considerate.....what happened to the land of justice, and constitutional rights....you let some militant cracker take you from the light........but is obvious you were already weak...you already enjoyed the night......so , where is the land of true emotion...is it hidden in the beheadings, the live burials, the burning cage......dear daughter, I am a marine and will always carry the rage........from the Philippines in the 70's, they have not stopped and been allowed to kill Christian people, 40 countries now....and where is the sound , the bell, in the church steeple.........if you don't like freedom from sharia and holy warriors, I suggest you meet them on their sand......because it we be over my dead body you take over this land......where are the babbling brooks, the music, the drink, politicians have always been greedy and pissed us down the sink......so jenny ,oh daughter of mine, do not judge me, it's the politicians who are blind......Sgt. ice rir

Grunt King

February 11 ·

Until you get rid of these demons and traitors of these United States.....the fascists are only stalling to cover up their tracks....kill'em all. Let God sort them out

Grunt King

February 11 ·

to the low heeled spark of the high heeled boy's, and my daughter Jenny......once upon a time in a land of love and true emotion....there was the collective, only for love and devotion....times were eventful, all the souls sored, only for the collective to get bored...it embraced itself to tightly, and the rules became unsound....it was the politics of the devil making his first round......divide and conquer, our favorite ploy,......only to act like it's never been used, but it still brings you joy....the ground is filled with warriors from all walks of life, the political , theocracies stalling and causing human strife......they come and they go with only one thing in mind, to kill all Christians, who have been so kind.....who are these holy warriors, Satanists, and scientology.....illiterates....their fraction from the collective is quite inconsiderate.....what happened to the land of justice, and constitutional rights....you let some militant cracker take you from the light........but is obvious you were already weak...you already enjoyed the night......so , where is the land of true emotion...is it hidden in the beheadings, the live burials, the burning cage......dear daughter, I am a marine and will always carry the rage........from the Philippines in the 70's, they have not stopped and been allowed to kill Christian people, 40 countries now....and where is the sound , the bell, in the church steeple.........if you don't like freedom from sharia and holy warriors, I suggest you meet them on their sand......because it we be over my dead body you take over this land......where are the babbling brooks, the music, the drink, politicians have always been greedy and pissed us down the sink......so jenny .oh daughter of mine, do not judge me, it's the politicians who are blind......Sgt. ice rir

Grunt King

February 12 · ·

Was that a little girl congratulating him and the 9th circuit? Even cried...

It...Even cried...

Grunt King

February 12 ·

And what the Seattle girly lawyer doesn't understand, under sharia...she, he's 1st

Grunt King

February 13 ·

Under Obama 1,000 illegals, on average, daily, + 3 mil deported in 8

Grunt King

February 13 ·

Including the average of 1000 illegals per-day, Obama also deported 3 mil

Grunt King

February 13 ·

The Obama admin. Allowed lawlessness to empower illegals and terrorists...

Grunt King

February 13 ·

Vista ca. home of transforming Mexican illegals into radical Muslims

Grunt King

To President Trump... it was the spring of 84, we were living behind live oak park on the other side of 395 on spring rd. we lived there with another military couple, guest house we sublet to another military couple. We had 6 acres to shoot our guns and bows. We had archery and pistol shooting contests, barbecues ...the works...my wife was pregnant. One day. It was a Saturday....we had company....we were watching an underground railroad....about 300 meters away....it just appeared...trucks by the 100's. They would hide themselves and the trucks in the barns....with my gear I analyzed their system. Every week there was a new batch......100's.....one day, I was on guard duty. Got a call from div. headquarters. When I arrived at my home it was surrounded by police and highway patrol.....my wife was being attended to by paramedics. All the screens were slashed, windows broken....I don't know how many of them were arrested. The highway patrolman looked at me and then my jeep. I had gone through 3 checkpoints, and I still had my m-16 in a military jeep. My side arm was still on....when I stopped shaking I asked what the hell is going on...he told me that each illegal pays 3,000 to an attorney in San Francisco, los angles, and so on. I ask him if there was anything he could do about it, and he said no. California politicians are behind it. it was a horrible scene.my wife sat there shaking, saying they were on the roof, the doors, the windows and by herself in what she thought was America....not so........fascist entity maybe.......Matt was a c - section, mike died 4 months later of c.i.d.s........a scene I will not forget. The underground moved. We moved to Fallbrook and the law continued to be broken to transform ca. into a fascist state. The illegals took it all....if you wanted a job Inca. They only wanted to pay you cash. Facebook is making this really hard to write. The illegals replaced white middle class Christians.............illegals ....suck what I got dangling...Sgt. Ice iir

Grunt King

February 14 ·

I say let's hang the son of a whore. Hang him and his militant shadow party. Hang all fascist......imagine if jihad Hillary would have won. But God would have none of it....

Obama Embraces 'Death Panel' Concept in Medicare Rule

During the stormy debate over his healthcare plan, President Barack Obama promised his program would not pull the plug on grandma, and Congress dropped plans for death panels and end of life counseling that...

Grunt King

February 14 ·

Zionists chuck Schumer has a wonderful chip and new retina, fingerprint ID

Grunt King

February 14 ·

Go to Jew news to learn more about chuck the mossad Schumer. Fuck off

Grunt King

February 14 ·

I have lived on the other side of martial law...this time I'm on the right side. You

Grunt King

February 22 ·

To President TRUMP AND FOX news
don't give socialist/ fascist Media any more publicity. We want the news. No more bitching, whining. FOX NEWS GROWS UP. REPORT NEWS ONLY!
Nobody cares about ABC, CNN ......Their News station than THEM.

Let their news station die like Obama care. Sit back let it self-destruct. If we want to hear what they have to say, we would listen to their news station. We are tired of BILDERBERGER playing Good Cops, BAD Cops.

Some Vietnam vets were never welcomed home

'Share' this to say "Your sacrifice is not forgotten"

Grunt King

February 23

you were bornin1991.no qualifications, just like everyone else in that son of a whores administration, Muslim brotherhood sucking Bilderberger cock.....and you were one of the traitors keeping your people in communication down from the sit. Room...fuck you jihad. Get out!

Rumana Ahmed: 5 Fast Facts You Need to Know

Rumana Ahmed is a Muslim and former National Security Council advisor in the White House. She wrote about her eight…

March 22 ·

Living in the land of old, dealing with the land of new...............

Grunt King

April 3 ·

clandestine meeting with Hillary Clinton at Bilderberg member Diane Feinstein's house at the time Bilderberg members were congregating only a few miles away.............the cunt is a heathen ...lock her up............

Bilderberg Feinstein; Dodd - China's Kadeer

Alternative News and Views, Reported by Agents around the World, 24 hours a day

Grunt King

April 5 ·

Barrack Hussein Obama aka Barry Soetoro...is an international criminal.

Tahiti is where the illiterate monkey Obama is...international criminal

If MUM core was reinstated there would be no international criminals. Expendable

Grunt King

April 17 ·

There are more republicans in the Democratic Party than democrats

R.I.P. America !!! You went soft on discipline. You raised the cost of living so high that both parents are always at work, rather than spending time with their children. You took God out of schools. Parents were told 'No you can't discipline your kids'. Kids have rights blah, blah, blah. Well. America!! You shall reap what you sow, we have lost generations of offspring that have turned into selfish, disrespectful brats who have no respect for people, property or authority! Things need to change! Copy & paste if you have the guts too!!! Give me an Amen if you agree.....! I am curious to see how many of my friends will agree with this.
Amen.

Grunt King

Orange suits are waiting.................Barry....your republicans ...I mean fascists are losing ground........your fascists are losing ground....the Bilderbergers are going down......Trump time.....hammer time, you son of a whore........aw...i'm a white woman with communist parents, and I only fuck black fascists and communists.....and our electorate voted twice to bring America down....twice for that cock sucking......low life....henry Kissinger die already....and for you younger Bilderbergers......you can't hide........we know where all of you live........SGT. ICE RIR

Susan rice, the Clintons, Loretta the genocide lynch....on and on.......we are going to fuck you for all your crimes..........you don't deserve to live.......kill'em all, let God sort them out.............General Westmoreland..............hang' em high

Grunt King

Susan Rice is a Bilderberger CUNT.....NAZI.....just ask your computer if Susan rice is a Bilderberger.....................go ahead snowflakes......fascists................know your illusion.....

Grunt King

Another DEMON...........fucks you....you globalist pansy ...America First, and don't you and McCain forget it......you're not republicans........your PUSSIES............FASCISTS...............obstructionists........you voted for Jihad Hillary........................

Grunt King

May 7 ·

· credibility....................Ms. Rice.............how did you receive 40,000,000$...........I'm a retired civil servant......I can't even have a vending co. ....it is in writing..........die cunt die we pray for your death in this manipulated Holy War.............................

Grunt King

May 4

Kambale Musavuli: Susan Rice's record on Africa suggests as Secretary of State, she would side with dictators and US allies Rwanda and Uganda against the people of Congo

Grunt King

May 7 ·

We are praying for your death.......especially the vet's.....we want you and your family.................to suffer like us.....we're dead already......when you went down, you should have taken the pill.........................

Barack Obama's administration has decided to get real tough in the past week now that his rule is coming to an end. In the span of less than a week, he has managed to piss of Israel and Russia. The expulsion of Russian...

Grunt King

May 20 ·

Kill them kill them all..............it is an illusion for control....seize
their bank accounts and pay for the wall...............

This morning at Casa Santa Marta, the current papal residence, Pope Francis
once more made his case against those who are clinging to the Laws of God,
claiming that they might lead a double life, are sick or are otherwise distorted.
.

Grunt King

May 24 ·

Orange jumpsuits......................Nuremburg...............trials must
begin!

Western liberals, reactionary evangelicals, and capitalist carpetbaggers alike
tout Paul Kagame as the herald of a new, self-reliant African prosperity."

You can take climate change, and stick it up your ass. America
would lose everything........like TPP....America 1st President
Trump........Tell them we're going to be the richest country...your
daughter, and son-in- law need to know their roll.....hire me...I will
show you how to leave politics out of everything. I am an
expert........you remember me........I ask to be your campaign
manager....you shouldn't have let Barry mac you...you should have
got rid of 17 Intel agencies, all fascists.......all Bilderberger
appointees, from the beginning....all from Barry....you could have
had it all............and if your daughter is in favor of the Paris climate
accord.....well, we know where she stands and "we want nothing to
do with her.....I have never voted...but I am more intelligent than a
politician..........I don't believe in politics...it is an illusion.....man-
made.....epidemic...airborne quasi-virus escaped from Franco-Arab
military labs, possibly potentiated by pollutants. It changed only the
reproductive cells, creating sterility........in men........leaving only
women to rule....CIA future......Sgt. Ice rir

Grunt King

May 28 ·

Nancy Pelosi is a cunt.........you should be hung by the neck until pronounced dead....it is coming little cunt trader.........where are those biological-non-bid-labs at ....cunt.....if I have to arrest you myself..........Bilderbergers can't save you........no one can save you your mansions are penetrable.......Sgt Ice Mum corps

Grunt King

May 28 ·

time................is going away........demons like Nancy Pelosi Soros, Rothschild Rockefeller ....all these demon teachers and there trust - fund babies.-may all Bilderbergers die so we as a world can live on in peace....they make the wars...they design who lives and dies.........die Nancy die you fucking cut

Grunt King

June 1 ·

We need to take offense

Grunt King

June 8 ·

Your jimmy the cleaner -I 'm Jimmy the Mail........your nothing but a little cunt, trying to continue Bush's world order,.....meet me in Yosemite Valley ...we got something for you boy, for insulting us with this dribble on a regular basis.......you like your family, boy ?...we like ours too.....me and you ...man-no to bitch.....what an embarrassment and failure ....we suggest the Bilderbergers get out of the way of progress or ....we won't fail...........unlike little bitch comey......we are professionals MUM CORPS

Grunt King

June 8 ·

James comey....ask your computer if he is a Bilderberger. The FBI will not

Grunt King

June 8 ·

It I a simple world ....1% vs. 99%, they're the ones that didn't earn their money......trust-fund-babies, ...bank of England. I mean bank of Rothschild.....

Grunt King

June 10 ·

Jerry brown, pussy, you are only a Gov. an illusion. MUM CORPS

Grunt King

June 10 ·

jerry, the cunt brown, 2018 loser, ca. fascist, 2020 loser....Ca. Regulators..

Grunt King

June 10 ·

Jerry browns a cunt Nancy Pelosi, a cunt, Feinstein, cunt MUM CORPS

Grunt King

June 10 ·

5,000,000 militia vs Bilderbergers..................we will show know mercy,....jerry, Nancy, soro's Schumer,..............etc. we have every name on file....turn-about-fair-play

California Enacts Laws Attacking Second Amendment » Alex Jones' Info wars: There's a war on for your mind!

Grunt King

June 11 ·

FOX, ABC, NBC, MSNBC, and RT>>>>>get your head out of your ass and report this................................

Jihad Escalates in the Philippines

By Christopher W. Holton Here at Terror Trends Bulletin, we have periodically reported on Jihadist groups and activities in the Philippines. This is a theater in the global jihad that is largely ...

Grunt King

June 12 ·

Barry said he was from Chicago, jihad Hillary said she was from where, ill.....?Not New York gives me a break

Donald Trump: 'Hillary, she's not a New Yorker!'

Donald Trump, resurfacing attacks hurled against Hillary Clinton during her Senate campaign, argued that the Democratic presidential nominee is "not a New Yorker" while speaking at an event hosted by the New York State Conservative Party.

Grunt King

June 12 ·

comey no credibility.....Mueller ....no credibility.... Bilderbergers way of obstruction, while the President tries to HELP America..............

Democrats Hit Back at FBI Chief Comey as Trump Presses Attacks on Hillary

Republican presidential nominee Donald Trump pressed his attack on Democratic rival Hillary Clinton's integrity as she struggled to get past a new firestorm over her emails...

Grunt King

June 12 ·

Sgt. King....sheamus mc Cray, Sgt. Ice, nick-names....1/9 78-79, 2531, BLT. Operator for C. CO. Col. Deforest, Capt. Leply, Capt. Guiney....Di-BO-Chet

Members of the infamous 1/9 Marines also referred to as "The Walking Dead"

Grunt King

June 13 ·

President Trump : Do what you have to do.....Barry caused this.....communist insurgency , Muslim insurgency, is against the Constitution....Barry's first 14 confirmations were Bilderbergers ....extract all Barry's appointments......we have put up with this for too long.....Sgt. ICE RIR

Grunt King

June 13 ·

If jihad Hillary would have won..........we would be under Martial law.......extract jihadists, communists.....under Pres. Trump.....under Hillary, it would have been Christians......do not let the demons steal our Thunder

Grunt King

June 13 ·

Go ahead ......we will round up all jihadists, communists, fascists, Loretta has already ordered the blades and the bags......they were meant for us.......turn-about-fair - play

Grunt King

June 13 ·

we are going to fuck you Barry Soetoro.....but not how you like it......orange jump-suits.........I want to be the one ....but I'm retired.....to extract Intel from you.......son of a whore

Obama Signs Executive Order Permanently Implementing Martial Law

Last Friday Obama made good on his promise to use executive action to expand his authority and quietly signed the ...

Grunt King

June 13 ·

Demons and reptiles..................
CIA And Satanism -

A powerful presentation on the subject by retired FBI agent Ted Gunderson.

Grunt King

June 13 ·

Wake up
Ted Gunderson FBI Whistleblower Killed By the Illuminati

Ted Gunderson was an Ex-FBI Chief whistleblower. He exposed Satanism in the CIA, drug running, chemtrails, the illuminati, my ultra-mind control. He was killed...

Grunt King

June 13 ·

Hey Schumer............you should have married a lizard from hotel ca. your wife is butt ugly..................
Grunt King
June 13 ·

Great story............funny and sad

Jewish people are not the real descendants of biblical Israel. Jews controlled African Slavery

Dr. Tony Martin and David Irving. The Jewish Role in the African Atlantic Slave Trade.

...

Grunt King

June 13 ·

We love you Mr. President.....Grunt gives you a high paw......

President Trump Exposes The Satanic Illuminati New World Order!! 2016

I sure hope he puts his money where his mouth is. I love what he had to say, and how he targeted the REAL issues. This is why he won. The truth always wins. ...

Grunt King

June 13 ·

Someone had to

PUTIN just brought the ROTHSCHILD WORLD SYSTEM to their knees

....

Grunt King

June 13 ·

Well, well

Boxcars with Shackles ordered for US Death Camps by FEMA

This story has been around for a bit but it's confirmed. FEMA has ordered 102,000 boxcars with shackles for detaining fighters, runners and other person's

Grunt King

June 14 ·

If any more of you fascists want to shoot someone. I live in Groveland ca.

Grunt King

June 14 ·

I helped run Bellville for years....obviously people have changed......thanks Barry

Grunt King

June 14 ·

Lawyers, Guns, and Money...Warren Zevon............

Grunt King

June 14 ·

Well, well
Why does the US Government need/have 30,000 Guillotines, and over 600 Million rounds of hollow point bullets?

Grunt King

June 14 ·

Evil is done in the darkness..............good is done in the Sunshine

Grunt King

June 14 ·

Well, well

Obama orders GUILLOTINES project End Game - documentation

DEATH camp and execution field documented in Arizona. Fema camp fema vans and prison facility on Mexico Arizona border. Obama signs executive orders aimed at the…

Grunt King

June 15 ·

Type, FBI Robert Mueller, doe's he represents the illuminati? Click-Donald j. drump, Robert mueller111-the hands of the dark. yes it says drump.click- Robert Mueller, prosecutor of the poor, defender of the rich. Click-25+best ideas about FBI chief on interest /illuminati...................................

Obama Admin Blocked FBI Director's Offer to Reveal Russian Meddling

Grunt King

June 17 ·

Well well

VETERANS ADMINISTRATION AND GANGSTALKING - NWO CIA VA MIND CONTROL, Brookhaven Labs, MONTAUK PROJECT

Grunt King

June 17 ·

Really....................yes........the V.A. number 1 in disarming America.......

Veterans Now Public Enemy Number One

the fact that the US military & international troops are training with local police for a possible response to a "Threat from Veterans" ..
YOUTUBE.COM

Knowledge...
Grunt King
June 17 ·

Angels in the middle..............DEMONS ON THE OUTSIDE......orange jumpsuits.....Barry and chimp

Obama's Shadow Government Is Organizing to Undermine Trump

The leaks that led to Michael Flynn's resignation are just the beginning. Obama and his loyalists in and outside government are working to undermine Trump.

Grunt King

June 17 ·

Barry soetoro was just the CEO of America, subterranean Gov. in control

Grunt King

June 17 ·

The Depopulation Storm to Bring In the NWO

Grunt King

June 18 ·

Nancy Pelosi, 2006 winner of the baby Christian eating contest....Zionist cunt

Grunt King

June 18 ·

you and Pelosi are CUNTS.......you should leave the country, hang with al Jazeera, your insight violence boy in America, punk......bank roll terrorism, you should be dropped off at the San Quinton PRISON YARD for a proper fuck......Nancy....you and the illuminati are Godless....fuck jeh-bull-on, the golden dawn, Zionism, luciferism, luciferian, jah-buh-lun, Jehovah God at low breath...............jao-bull-on , jao-bel-aun.......jah-bul-aum, we want

109

out of the NWO....................and fuck the subterranean 's
................DO NOT VOTE FOR THIS CUNT....................SGT.
ICE RIR........................

Grunt King

June 18 ·

All fascists, Paul Ryan, ...Pelosi, Schumer, Kissinger, know all of
your names,...........above and below......stationed pt. mugu.....you
need to listen to this...............catching on................................?

Grunt King

June 18 ·

Almost 60...., musician, poet, engineer, plant, engineer, research
and development, retired civil service, disabled vet. my father said,
never be confused by someone you thought you knew.....oh yes.....I
used to help run a few town's.............my favorite band..........soul,
rhythm................blues all wrapped up in
one...

Talking Heads - Once in a Lifetime LIVE Los Angeles '83

Extra it de " Stop Making Sense " realize par Jonathan Demme (sorti en 1984
), à partier images de concerts des Talking Heads au Hollywood's Pant ages
Theater...

Grunt King
June 19 ·

Illuminati............................move over, there is a NEW SHERRIFF
in DC..........Pelosi..........it's getting about that time.....................

NEWT GINGRICH CONFIRMS 'TRUMP IS NOT SECRET SOCIETY!'

Donald Trump does not belong to any secret societies, he is not a Satanist like
the Bush' or the Clinton's and that is why they are trying to thwart his run...

Grunt King

June 19 ·

Well------------------------........................ wondered what happened to music............I play a twelve and six beautifully, they don't want me....

The Tall Israeli That Runs the Rap Industry - Illuminati Satanic Music Industry Exposed

Lyor Cohen has been actively involved in hip-hop at various top labels for more than 30 years. But how…

Grunt King

June 19 ·

We have known forever.................my father told me.............my uncle is worth..............b................

ILLUMINATI Bloodlines of Deception 1 RELOADED Obama, Bush, Egypt, Politics, Evil

Grunt King

June 19 ·

President Trump..............sir he thinks were GOYIM. Please stop this ....SGT. ICE.................RIR

Mueller and Comey- American Crime Brothers Exposed

Thomas and Betsy discuss the appointment of Robert Muller as Special Council to oversee the Trump-Russia "witch-hunt

Grunt King

June 19 ·

What does the next Bilderberg meeting have in common with an F-35?

Grunt King

June 19 ·

Year 1140, 0 lodges, Scotland, mother Lodge.........

Grunt King

June 19 ·

We performed this acoustically on the corner of sunset and vine Dec. 77..................

The Doors - The End (original)

...

Grunt King

June 20 ·

No shit

Veteran's scandal risks engulfing Obama

Amid contrived outrage over Benghazi and the improving fortunes of its healthcare reform, the Obama administration could be facing a genuine scandal about its treatment of military veterans that ha...

Grunt King

June 20 ·

To Jon Ossoff..........hides the fact that his co. works with al Jazeera, the terrorist sympathizing network that served as the mouthpiece of Osama bin laden. ossoff personally made more than 5,000$ from al Jazeera even though they have a history of inciting anti- American violence throughout the Muslim world and their backers have been accused of bankrolling terrorists-what a little punk....sounds like these fascists in ca.spreading like a disease. Do you think you will last CUNT- ask baby -eating Pelosi how bright her future is...........Paul Ryan.............your next......SGT. ICE RIR...........

Grunt King

June 22 ·

Get-out...........................we will protect our own first...........out..................now

Grunt King

June 22

·

Get out, out......................Luciferians.....no more demons allowed..................

Grunt King

June 22 ·

get out...............we have or own to take care of...............we want people with soul.................a good soul.............if you have a good soul...get in line............no more illuminati tricks.............to enslave America................n's....we built this bitch , and we going to enjoy it...........

Immigration 101: Will illegal immigrants now have health coverage?

President Obama will deny health benefits to the 5 million people he is shielding from deportation. But these undocumented immigrants have other ways of getting health...

Grunt King

June 22 ·

Paul Ryan, Soros, luciferians, reinstate Barry soetoro, and you will be sorry. I tried to tell you............there is no party.......and fuck you mc Cain...illuminati punk....

Clinton Insider Leaks, "They Plan To Impeach Trump In 6 Months" Guess Who They Have In Waiting...

Grunt King

June 23 ·

Ugly bitch...............you lose Luciferians....................

Ever See, Michelle Obama, AKA,"Big Mike," In A Bathing Suit?

I could not find a single picture of him in a bathing suit, have you?

Grunt King

June 23 ·

the holy war is between the Christians and the Luciferians...............you and other imposter............get out of our country....with rest of the Zionists........

Obama Mocks & Attacks Jesus Christ And the Bible / Video / Obama Is Not A Christian

Obama Mocks and Attacks Jesus Christ and the Bible. A top U.S. evangelical leader is accusing Sen. Barack...

June 28 ·

REMEMBER.....................Have you ever noticed the strategic attrition age for males...............in America.................and other countries? Tomorrow we'll talk about the illuminati and their Muslim front country acquisitions.................................

Killing People1975-1979

Genocide in Cambodia (1975-1979) By April 1975, a Communist group known as the Khmer Rouge, led by Pol Pot, seized control of Cambodia...

Grunt King

June 28 ·

they have been around for a while............right Kissinger..............Rothschild, Soros, Clinton's and well, you know.................Nimrod...............before Flood...Jesuit element.....etc. ....

The FREEMASON'S SECRET KEY is SODOMY

WARNING!! VERY DARK MATERIAL - TRIGGER WARNING.
Freemasons Secret Brotherhoods' definition of Success is Sodomizing Children before the age of 4 years.

Grunt King
June 28 ·

Holly..WOOD...........JEWWOOD....
....

The Satanic Illuminati in Hollywood! (2017 WARNING)

Grunt King

June 29 ·

You're not just catching up?

Grunt King

June 29 ·

Really.............Barry

ROTHSCHILD HUMILIATES OBAMA, "AMERICA is WORLD's BIGGEST TAX HAVEN" Panama Papers.

ROTHSCHILD HUMILIATES OBAMA, "AMERICA is...

Grunt King

June 30 ·

It doesn't matter who the people vote for, because they always vote for US............Joseph Stalin.............ILLUMINATI...

Illuminati Hand Signs and Handshakes - Ron Paul

You'd think Ronnie Paul would know better... and why would Ron Paul's YouTube campaign site run a subliminal message of Saddam Hussein's face??? At: 45 second...

Grunt King

June 30 ·

come up to Groveland Ca. Bill..........we have something for you...........you Luciferian FUCK...........................SGT. ICE RIR...............................

Bill Maher the Zionist

He doesn't believe in religion but he supports Israel just so that his masters (Zionists) will be happy with him. Never seen him speak against Judaism have u...

116

Grunt King

June 30 ·

Money will not save you. You never worked in the mountains. You never worked in the tunnels..................you're a glitch in time..........LUCIFERIAN..................poor little Billy............

Christian Bullshit Nailed by Bill Maher - Antitheist Atheist

Grunt King

June 30 ·

You're right..............you are the illuminati house......................................

Bill Maher Racist joke ("I'm a house nigger")

Bill Maher tells a very racist joke, calling himself a house nigger.

Grunt King

June 30 ·

Mika..............I play a 12 string.....you want to see my hands...? Your punk-lizard DAD................cunt

BRZEZINSKI THE REAL ZIONIST REPTILIAN

Grunt King

June 30 ·

Life during their WARTIME..................their chosen WARS..........................not ours.................LIZARD-KINGS.................hi Jenny...........

The Serpent Bloodline: Ebonite/Khazar Jews and Sons of Cain | Truth Control

117

There are several deceptions in the churches today and one of the most dominant is that Zionism …

Grunt King added a new photo to the album

: Grunt…………

July 3 ·

July 3 ·

If you haven't been taught history, how can you learn from it? Fireworks and all…………………

Mercedes #1

The lyric addresses aspects of the Killing Fields and Year Zero but also the radically changed lives of the children of Cambodian refugees

Greg Lavender 1959-2013……best unknown guitar player………………God rests your Soul………………

AC/DC - Who Made Who

Grunt King

42 percent of new Medicaid sign-ups are illegals....Medicaid helps hospitals pay for illegal care...3.1 million illegals are receiving 8.1 billion annually, taxpayers cost, 4.3 billion annually. Illegals and their children benefit more than documented personnel.........get out of our country..........now.......you fascist Luciferians can go with them.....my claim is in the V.A DOR..............if you don't grant it my civil attorney's will put their fist so far up your ass you'll wish you burned as a child................not to mention Palo Alto and La Jolla............We are planning................you are attrition driven demons.....you just want to kill the people you can't control...............like Anglo-Saxon's, with an 120 I.Q. and over...................................

More than $91.6 million in Medicare payments went to services for illegal aliens in recent years

Medicare payments to health care providers for services rendered to illegal aliens totaled more than $91.6 million from 2009 to 2011

Grunt King

July 11 ·

If your "new's" channels can't deliver, and then say good-bye ratings..............

Bombshell: Hillary Clinton's Ties to Russia Could Topple US Government

Putin was left "astonished" after Trump presented evidence at G20 showing how Hillary Clinton had penetrated the Russian government.

Grunt King

July 11 ·

Good-bye illuminati news..........................

119

Enormity of Hillary Clinton Penetration into Russia Warned Could Topple US Government

A gravely toned Security Council (SC) report circulating in the Kremlin today states that President Putin was "astonished/amazed" after President Donald Trump...

Grunt King

July 11 ·

Clinton foundation........................illuminati front.......poor little jumpsuits are waiting...........

Senate Panel to Hear Testimony from Businessman Targeted By Trump Dossier Firm

A London-based businessman who was investigated last year by the opposition research firm behind the so-called Trump dossier will testify before the Senate...

Grunt King

July 13 ·

We are the true Warriors.....................don't forget it..............imagine, if you would have had the courtesy to stay where you belonged you're the uncivilized ones. You are heathens for love of the BEAST...........money.......nothings never enough. The Luciferians were beaten and put back in the ground. and you weak Bilderbergers............had to make a deal with the devil........love for technology...........MONEY...........an illusion......your laws will be soon forgotten.....they are artificial........controlling........because there are only a few of you...........why in the HELL would you want LAWYERS doing anything for you, except the obvious. Bank of Rothschild............give me a break...........bank of anything. Take your money out and start your own bank with your friends...............................Washington dc....................what a joke...........there are no parties.................the U.S. ....Bilderbergers and henry Kissinger is responsible ....SGT.ICE RIR..

120

Native Veterans Day 2006 online

Native America series NATIVE VETERANS DAY 2006 On November 10, 2006, Native American veterans from around the country met at Chukchansi Park in Fresno.

.

Grunt King
July 18 ·
YouTube

.

Our generation was cool as hell.................pimping hard.......it moved your mind, not stifled it.................................

Grunt King

July 19 ·
Marine Boot-camp......Sgt. Ice RIR

July 19 ·

Time to go

we are going to fuck all of you one way or the
other..................you'll wish you died as a child...............you know
where we live and vice -versa..........

Former Obama Administration Staffers Now Making Money off Obama care

Dozens of former Obama staffers who wrote and implemented Obama care are
now "cashing in" on the...

Grunt King

July 26 ·

To the broken families...............and the hell with illegal
Medicaid...........get them out so "you" can help us.

Tips for making money from Obama care (until it goes bankrupt)

Because it looks like we're stuck with Obama care (unless Chief Justice
Roberts grows tired of media adulation before other constitutional challenges to
the law reach the Supreme Court), here are some
DAILYCALLER.COM

Grunt King

July 27 ·
News Punch

former illuminati, the cunt Schultz, will pay a dear price
soon.............children of the corn are going down...................when
we arrested demons, we started at the finish line..........Sessions ,
start in D.C. and work your way out......the easiest way...political
correctness is gone. Get to it................Sgt. Ice RIR

Grunt King

July 27 ·

To the low spark of high heeled boys... she sat there for hours it
seemed, not really noticing the time, or time of day for that matter.
Doris looked around the room, realizing this was it, the time she
thought she was waiting for. The room was bright as it always was
this time of day, one last look around, for the road Doris said to
herself. She picked up her suitcases and headed for the door,
banging everything on the way out, knocking the door wide open,
and almost falling in the hallway. Suddenly, Doris lost her breath,
focusing on the object on the stairs between the railings. It was her
Wedding Ring. The buzzer started to ring downstairs; it was her
future husband Diane. The buzzer kept ringing, and Doris went
numb, finally getting up, she went back inside her apartment,
opened the window, knocked out the screen and began shouting "I

DON'T LIKE TACOS ", I really don't like tacos....Doris looked
down at Diane and said , I just don't like tacos........Sgt. Ice
RIR........Richard Pryor allowed us to make fun of ourselves.....i
suggest we take the late Great Comics advice.........Richard would
have beat down Billy Maher anyway.....they even politicked
comedy for p.c. ....come back Richard Pryors, we need you...

Grunt King

July 27 ·

To the President......Tell Henry Kissinger enough is enough. We
know there's no party...ok......we know you're surrounded and pray
for you and your family. I asked your Wife, the 1st Lady to keep a
CIA eye on you a while ago. We know the American Bilderbergers
from the center of America lowered their hammer. Just tonight
people said you were not supposed to win.............I 'm sorry I don't
have respect for illusionist. Democrats go to D.C. to make money.
Republicans go to D.C. to make money. President Trump went to
D.C. to make us, you money...............Sgt. Ice RIR

These Nine Republicans Voted Against the Latest Repeal, Replace Amendment

Hours after the Senate voted to begin debate on their healthcare overhaul, an
amendment that would repeal Obama care and replace it with a more restrictive
plan...

Grunt King

July 28 ·

IF WE HERE BARRY- CARE ONE MORE TIME........SGT. ICE RIR

Grunt King

July 28 ·

President Trump: why in the hell do you allow taxpayers to pay this SOB's protection, his salary when you know he's guilty of treason, murder, collusion, espionage, etc. "WE" have a feeling, this won't do......SGT. ICE RIR

Mia Marie Pope Ousts Barack Obama as a Foreigner

Mia Marie Pope, who was a high school friend of Barack Obama (aka Barry Soetoro) in Hawaii…

Grunt King

July 28 ·

Barry soetoro is a punk and should be tortured and locked up indefinitely.........

BREAKING: Whistleblower Exposes Obama's Sickening Crime against Veterans

Barack Obama did many disgusting things during his time as president. Among the most sickening was his horrible treatment of our veterans.

Grunt King

July 30 ·

You shouldn't have to be a 33, or corporate agent, high brass, collaborator, grey, Nordic, the Queen or FOX news to ride this bitch. We are tired of flying. Those magnetic trains go "fast". I loved working out of the mountains of Ojai. ....SGT. ICE RIR

Grunt King

July 30 ·

All day and all night.................the park is working

UFO Yosemite Park near Area 51

Grunt King

July 30 ·

There is a place for Demons like this Lizard...........SGT. ICE RIR...

Grunt King

July 31 ·

Yes, I'm sending this again. The severity of nature, and the problems and deaths across the world this Obama supporter and traitor must be dealt with in a functional play by play manner of which the investigation must be handled. This SOB ruined lives, caused suicides just like the ...... did. He killed people by being an emotionless SWINE. by kicking us in the teeth every day for believing in our constitution....and this low down punk extended it....You Know Mr. President.........your wrong ...he is not a good anything, and should be interrogated to the fullest measure. These are enemies, just like California, the entire state is a communist state. And they tried murdering me many times to get here.it is not just him. Who paid him? M.C. Cain...Soros, one of the many "republicans" on the communist side. you do realize that there are more communists in the house and senate than politicians..............how about, oh I know , everyone was in on it except the Trump administration............that's a lot of enemies....send the Marshals..........SGT. ICE RIR...

126

August 31 ·

Good morning grunt

Grunt King

September 2 at 9:56pm ·

every veteran from the Vietnam war and on will see you punished
by God all mighty, and I am not talking about Nordics and
Greys....you bunch of Luciferians.........fuck teddy Roosevelt...weak
soul...all of you ...you know........were coming...the mountains...

That's the crux of your problem traitor McCain - You don't answer
to anyone except John McCain. You flout the will of the American
people and Trump and your fellow Republican Senators. You just
need to go the way of another "Maverick," Chappaquiddick Ted.

Grunt King

September 2 at 10:57pm ·

If I die today Lord, send my Soul back, only to be a better Marine...

Grunt King

September 3

It is time for shock and aw.......Collaborators agree.....

September 3

This is my best childhood friend Dave Leach, if you believe in God, pray. If you just believe, Hope......Dave, Grunt and I have a lot of fishing to do. the caregiver and I are going to take a little trip...Grunt , management, has made the strategic arrangements...Maria C. Medeiros, I know your busy, but you can spread love over the world, you got what it takes. Eve, give up the prayers love. Everyone spread the news that vacation Dave is here to stay.

Vacation Dave updated his cover

Grunt King

September 3

You Luciferians do get it? , don't you? Nancy Pelosi, Henry Kissinger, john mc Cain, chucky the Israel spy, mich mc connel, imf, cfr, illuminati, Bilderbergers, 2% Zionists, greys Nordics.....times are a changing. Get on board with the Lord or the nourishment for the greys and their collaborators will rest literally on you. You will be given to them for food. The Nordics will receive the rest of you as science projects. Funny, you thought paper trees could save you. My soul sees everything...and for you Astro Beings.........enough is enough. Alright already. I know. Please do your research.

Grunt King

He is a Luciferian, mason-illuminati taking orders from city bank of London, Rothschild's bank. The cunt, queen of England and her band of mi-5, 6, CIA. . The CIA, like NASA is an individual entity, not part of anything, except to control us the Luciferians wishes. They control us through parties, like the democrats and republicans...there is no such thing...an illusion. We need to start at the top of the swamp "England", when the cunt "queen Bee dies", I know of over 5,000,000 that will be ecstatic. That's just me. wake - up ,please wake up, research, research......why do you think Hillary was ordered to bring in Jihadists, communist insurgents, Muslim insurgents, educating the Asians by giving them priority in universities in the US, OUR COUNTRY, . In 1954 they, the Bilderbergers decided on the US destruction. When I was in the Military I saw what the queen and the IMF, cfr, illuminati, Bilderbergers, militant pussies like Barry soetoro and big mike. I, SGT. ICE am damn sick of it...........do really think the Nordics want their planet blown up. Watch out for those Astro beings, it is very uncomfortable, when two spirits are within one body. My Uncle Austin Murray was a high ranking official in the Armed Forces, my father in - law was a 33. And not the first....I hung out at the Nights of Columbus when I was a kid serving sandwiches and drinks. I have been invited to many Lodges. But I am a Buddhist...

DO NOT BEND

The Committee for
The Presidential Inaugural
Washington, D.C. 20599

AUTO**5-DIGIT 95

The King Household

Groveland, CA 95321-9526

The Committee for
The Presidential Inaugural
requests the honor of your presence
to attend and participate in the Inauguration of

Donald John Trump

as President of the United States of America

and

Michael Richard Pence

as Vice President of the United States of America

on Friday, the twentieth of January

two thousand and seventeen

in the City of Washington

Presidential Inaugural Committee
Commemorative Invitation
1789-2017

On January 20, 2017, our nation honored the 58th inauguration of the President and Vice President of the United States of America. This special occasion celebrated the triumph of our democracy with a peaceful transition of power and the shared ideal that make its continuance possible.

Please accept this invitation as one gift to commemorate the inauguration of Donald John Trump as the 45th President of the United States of America and Michael Richard Pence as 48th Vice President of the United States of America.

The 58th Presidential Inaugural Committee
Thomas J. Barrack, Jr.
Chairman

Made in the USA
Middletown, DE
08 September 2024

60528007R00075